America Underfoot

HLM

America Underfoot

A History of Floor Coverings from Colonial Times to the Present

Anthony N. Landreau

Published for the
Smithsonian Institution Traveling Exhibition Service
by the Smithsonian Institution Press
Washington D.C.

1976

Library of Congress Cataloging in Publication Data
Landreau, Anthony N. 1930—
    America underfoot.

    Bibliography: p.
    1. Carpets—United States—Catalogs. 2. Rugs—
United States—Catalogs. I. Smithsonian Institution
Traveling Exhibition Service. II. Title.
NK2812.L36   746.7′074′013   76-608162

Contents

Preface

Prior to 1954 little had been written about floor coverings in America. The few exceptions were works on the development of the industry. Most notable were the writings of Arthur Harrison Cole. Joseph V. McMullan of New York, a well-known collector of Oriental rugs, provided an important breakthrough with his 1954 article, "The Turkey Carpet in Early America," in *Antiques* magazine. This report provided a clue to the study of the subject, made difficult by the dearth of examples, by showing the four early American paintings (there are now five) that depict Oriental rugs. McMullan's article was followed by two excellent historic studies in 1967: Nina Fletcher Little's *Floor Coverings in New England Before 1850* and Rodris Roth's *Floor Coverings in 18th-Century America*. Roth's study, with its thorough research of documents and paintings, has become the principal text on the subject. Other examples and information have since emerged. The next major breakthrough was in 1975 when Mildred B. Lanier published the catalog of *English and Oriental Carpets at Williamsburg*, a complete historic and technical survey of an important collection. As Lanier says on page 128, many questions "could be more accurately resolved if illustrations of the many carpets now reposing in museum storerooms were published."

Several other scholars whose works have not yet been published, notably Charles Hummel of The Henry Francis du Pont Winterthur Museum in Delaware and Virginia Partridge of the Farmers' Museum in Cooperstown, New York, have been important in developing the present body of knowledge. The report, currently in press, of the 1975 Irene Emery Roundtable on Textiles at The Textile Museum in Washington, D.C. includes papers by Hummel and Partridge.

The intent of this monograph is to bring the story of floor coverings up to date by summarizing the information from previous works and from lesser known sources and to introduce additional information.

The author is indebted to a great number of people for their help. I would like to express my appreciation to several persons in the Smithsonian Institution's National Museum of History and Technology—Rita Adrosko, curator of textiles, and Lois Vann, museum specialist, in the Division of Textiles, who were most helpful with preparations for the exhibition; and to Rodris Roth, curator in the Division of Costume and Furnishings.

Mildred Lanier of Colonial Williamsburg and Charles Hummel of Winterthur went beyond the "call of duty" to be helpful. Thomas Leavitt, Peter Molloy, and Katherine Koob of the Merrimack Valley Textile Museum, and Louise Mackie, Patricia Fiske, and Ann Hedlund of The Textile Museum in Washington, D.C., were most helpful, as were Mrs. Dexter Ferry, Ronald Miller, and Sarah McGhee of Natchez, Mississippi. Others I cannot omit are Leon Arkus, Museum of Art, Carnegie Institute; Verna Curtis, Milwaukee Art Center; James Fisher of Fisher Scientific Company; Ron Goodman, Washington, D.C.; Dennis Gould, director of SITES; Anne McKenrick of Floorcloths, Inc.; Marjorie Share of SITES; Sarah Sherrill of *Antiques* magazine; Paul Smith, Museum of Contemporary Crafts; and James Thomas of Pleasant Hill, Kentucky. I also wish to express my gratitude to all of the lenders to the exhibition and to the contributors of illustrations. The following institutions and individuals should be especially thanked for their contributions of rugs, technical advice, and financial support: The American Revolution Bicentennial Administration; Patcraft Mills, Inc.; Bigelow-Sanford, Inc.; Scalamandré; Floorcloths, Inc.; Smithsonian Institution; Colonial Williamsburg; Merrimack Valley Textile Museum; Museum of Natural History, Carnegie Institute; The Textile Museum, Washington, D.C.; Sylvia Spradlin; Urban Jupena; Glen Kaufman; and Marjorie Rhodes.

I could not end my list without drawing very special attention to those who have worked long and hard to assist me in the completion of this text: Quinton Hallett of SITES, without whose expert steering of the project 'twixt Scylla and Charybdis we would never have succeeded; my wife Anita for her editorial help and Marcella Henry for her expert typing; and Ruth Fisher, who is becoming well-known for her fine illustrations of Oriental rugs, for her drawings.

ANTHONY N. LANDREAU

Acknowledgments

The Smithsonian Institution Traveling Exhibition Service is very pleased to be circulating this important exhibition which documents over two hundred years of floor coverings in America. The generosity of the lenders and the participation of many who have supported the project since its embryonic stages have enabled us to present especially fine historical and contemporary examples of our floor-covering heritage.

Special credit should be given to Anthony N. Landreau for organizing the exhibition and supplying the text for this catalog. Mr. Landreau's dedication to the project and his cooperation throughout have produced commendable results.

There is always a group of people whose roles behind the scenes of an exhibition are essential, yet they often escape adequate recognition. I would like to express particular thanks to the following Smithsonian Institution colleagues who were most closely involved with *America Underfoot* and without whose contributions the exhibition would not be possible:

From SITES, Dennis A. Gould, director; Antonio Diez, administrative officer; Kathleen S. Hopkins, registrar; Marjorie L. Share, program coordinator; and Jane Murphy, intern. From the Smithsonian Office of Exhibits Central, Constance R. Minkin, chief exhibits editor, and Kenneth V. Young, assistant chief of design; and Gerard A. Valerio, designer.

QUINTON HALLETT

Exhibition Coordinator
Smithsonian Institution
Traveling Exhibition Service

Introduction

I f it is underfoot, is it beneath your attention? Look again! The floor covering that you may have taken for granted is part of a rich history involving sturdy pioneers, patriots, and presidents. It is not only part of America's folk-art culture, but also of the art history of the ancient East and Europe. This history encompasses great inventions and the emergence of a dynamic industry from humble handicraft beginnings. The story is still unfolding. With the development of the revolutionary tufted carpet in the mid-twentieth century, the American carpet industry, which outstripped its competitors in the mid-nineteenth century, is again leading the world in inventive genius and productivity. Look again at the whole world of history, art, and technology beneath your feet!

The purpose of this catalog, which accompanies the exhibition being circulated by the Smithsonian Institution Traveling Exhibition Service, is to bring together under one roof all of the knowledge of floor coverings in America. In that sense much of the material covered recapitulates the research reported in other texts, although some new information is also presented. The organization of material and unreferenced opinions are the author's responsibility.

Sand and Straw

Colonial Americans busy carving out a new continent had little time to enjoy such amenities as rugs on the floor. The floor of the farmer and the pioneer was of dirt. With unpaved roads and muddy boots in town as well as in the country, such luxurious items as rugs would have been totally unsuitable. Even in Europe, the Eastern notion of rugs on the floor had not caught on except among the most affluent. "In Europe the general run of houses were innocent of textile floor-coverings; though rushes, sand, and in some sections skins, served to collect the dirt, soften the tread, and protect the feet from the coldness of the floors."[1]

Sand was one solution. It absorbed moisture, was useful for cleanliness, and could even—if ephemerally—satisfy a need for decoration. Sand was reportedly used in mid-western log cabins well into the nineteenth century, and John F. Watson in the *Annals of Philadelphia* describes city sanded floors in the eighteenth century:

> *Turkey carpets were spoken of, and only to be seen upon the floors of the first families of wealth. Parlour floors of very respectable people in business used to be "swept and garnished" every morning with sand sifted through a "sand sieve," and sometimes smoothed with a hair broom, into quaint circles and fancy wreaths, agreeably to the "genius for drawing" possessed by the chambermaid.*[2]

William Wheeler advertised in the *Boston News-Letter* in 1746 that he had "scouring sand for Floors . . . . The Larger the Quantity the less the Price."[3]

The Old Sandman was much more than a fictional bedtime character for children—as attested by sand beneath the floors of many eighteenth-and nineteenth-century homes and by floors worn through from the abrasion of sand sweeping. Perhaps the sawdust floors popular in saloons even in the mid-twentieth century were a throwback to the sand era?

Straw matting also emerged as a floor covering in the eighteenth century (figure 1). The English and Continental custom of strewing the floor with rushes can be traced to the Middle Ages, when it extended even to royal use;[4] however, the eighteenth-century American use of woven straw matting apparently was "not closely associated" with this continental custom.[5] Most of the straw seems to have come from the East—from China, India, or East India. George Washington ordered straw matting "from China" for Mount Vernon.[6] Straw mats, referred to as Spanish, probably reflect a type of material such as Spanish rush, mat-weed, or feather grass rather than the country of origin.[7]

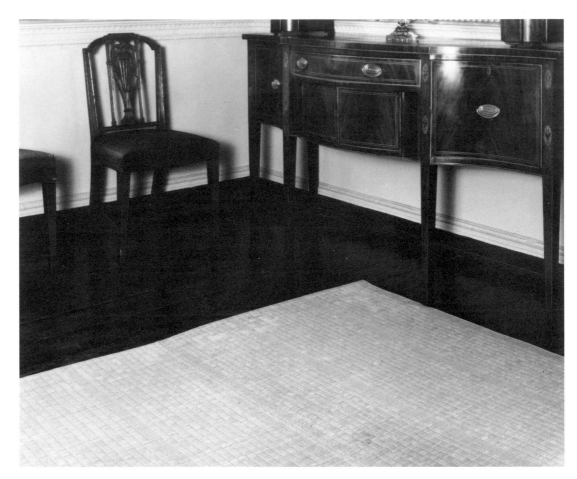

1. Straw matting on the floor at Mount Vernon. This matting is modern, obtained from Hong Kong, but thought to be similar to types mentioned in George Washington's inventories. (Courtesy of The Mount Vernon Ladies' Association of the Union. Photograph by Raymond Schwartz.)

Straw matting, however, had its limitations. Rejecting the idea of purchasing some for the White House dining room, Thomas Jefferson mentions the problems of wear and of soiling from grease.[8] Vermin posed another serious problem.

Straw matting was commonly used for entrances and hallways as well as bedrooms. As affluence increased and other types of floor coverings became popular, different uses were developed for matting, such as padding beneath woven carpets and as covers "to lay over carpets, particularly in summer."[9] Baize—coarsely woven wool or cotton—was also used as a covering for rugs.

To the dismay of a French visitor, Brissot de Warville, in 1788, Americans were quite ostentatious in their use of woven rugs.

> *It already appears: they have carpets, elegant carpets; it is a favourite taste with the Americans; they receive it from the interested avarice of their old masters the English.*
> *A carpet in summer is an absurdity; yet they spread them in this season, and from vanity: this vanity excuses itself by saying that the carpet is an ornament; that is to say, they sacrifice reason and utility to show.*[10]

This was not always the case, for many Americans apparently rolled their rugs for summer

or stored them in winter rooms. Some used straw matting in summer. Those who used floorcloths may have substituted lighter weight ones or used the cloths themselves as summer replacements for carpets. It is interesting to note that straw mats imported from the Orient have recently become fashionable again for covering the floor.

The specific construction of the matting used in colonial times is not known, although it probably varied widely. Many types imported today may be quite similar. In a letter to Thomas Jefferson, Thomas Claxton mentions straw matting "which is variegated in colour white and red . . . ."[11] The Bishop White house in Philadelphia has black plaid woven matting.

2. *The Sargent Family,* American, about 1800. Rodris Roth states: "The floors in these rooms are completely covered, the principal one with a large checkered pattern of brown, tan, and cream." (Courtesy of the National Gallery of Art, Washington, D.C., gift of Edgar William and Bernice Chrysler Garbisch.)

3. Trade card of Alexander Wetherstone, English, about 1760, who among other items sold list carpets and painted floorcloths. (Courtesy of the British Museum, Sir Ambrose Heal Collection.)

4. From "Floor-Decorations of Various Kinds . . . Adapted to the Ornamenting of Halls, Rooms, Summerhouses, &c. . . ." Designed and engraved by John Carwitham, London, 1739, plate 8. Additional Carwitham plates are illustrated in Roth, 1967, and in Comstock, 1955. Little, 1967, illustrates other English trade card and floorcloth patterns, in figure 17. (Courtesy of the Library of Congress.)

I. Carwitham Inv. et sc. 1739.

Painted Floors and Floorcloths

As Americans became wealthier, in the eighteenth century, they acquired a taste for the woven rugs that were becoming popular abroad. These came within reach of middle-class America as hardwood floors emerged—along with burgeoning industrial capability and the protective tariffs of the 1820s and 1830s. Rugs of all types, except homemade, had been scarce, especially the precious Oriental and English varieties. In addition, the rich tile and marble patterns of European and Asian floors were much admired.

Various types of painted substitutions developed: painting and, by the early nineteenth century, stenciling directly on the floor in imitation of rugs, parquet floors, and marble and tile patterns. Mrs. Ruth Henshaw, a minister's wife in Fitzwilliam, New Hampshire, painted the parsonage floor to imitate a plain striped carpet.[12] Floors, along with walls and other areas meant for decoration, were frequently ornamented by itinerant painters. Parts of such floors, hidden under furniture and carpeting, have survived.[13]

Floor oilcloths were introduced from England in the early eighteenth century. Painted floors, having the disadvantage of being stationary, may have been an adaptation of floorcloths—or they may have developed simultaneously. Stenciling and block-printing techniques evolved from hand-painting in eighteenth-century England.

To produce an oilcloth, several layers of oil paint were applied to woven cloth. The top layer might be plain or decorated. The woven cloth was usually heavy and durable, such as canvas, although lighter cloths were sometimes used in summer or when the cloth was intended as a cover for a carpet. When used on the floor, oilcloths were frequently referred to as floorcloths.

Oilcloths can be traced to fourteenth-century France where painted hangings and tablecovers were used.[14] There is evidence of a brisk manufacture of oilcloths for floors in eighteenth-century England (figures 3 and 4). Contemporary inventories and advertisements indicate that oilcloths were primarily imported into the colonies at first. In fact, before the American Revolution, there was a great deal of prestige in having imported goods.[15] Evidence of local pride appears after mid-century, as indicated by this advertisement of May 10, 1786, in the Charleston *South Carolina Gazette and Country Journal.*

WAYNE & RUGER, Painters & Glaziers, Take this Method of informing the Public, that they have opened a Shop on the Bay . . . where they carry on the House and

Ship-Painting Business, in all its Branches; Signs and Floor Cloths, painted as neat as any from London, Gilding, Japanning, Glazing, etc., etc.[16]

In eighteenth-century America, the manufacture of floorcloths was a lively business, although cloths were also made at home. Itinerant painters were active in rural areas.[17] A class of painters of floors, coaches, houses, and signs developed. Upholsterers and paper-hangers also got into the oilcloth business in the cities. Indentured servants often provided the skilled labor, as evidenced by an advertisement in the Annapolis *Maryland Gazette*, June 26, 1760: "Run away from the Subscriber, a convict servant man named John Winters, a very compleat House Painter; he can imitate marble or mahogany very exactly, and can paint Floor Cloths as neat as any imported from Britain."[18]

In the United States, oilcloths may have been used on the floor slightly earlier than Oriental rugs, which first were table coverings. The first mention of oilcloths is in the 1729 inventory of the estate of William Burnet, governor of New York, New Jersey, and finally Massachusetts. The second is the inventory in 1732 at the death of Robert "King" Carter of Virginia.[19]

Painted floors and floorcloths may have first been of interest as imitations of the rugs and floors of Europe and Asia, but came to be highly regarded for their own sakes. Their appearance in eighteenth- and nineteenth-century portraits is a clue to their esteem. In addition to Carter and Williams, at least three presidents were among the prominent Americans who used floorcloths—George Washington, John Adams, and Thomas Jefferson. President Jefferson had plain green painted cloth in the south dining room of the White House. There is also evidence that floorcloths were sometimes given equal billing with rugs in their household position.[20]

Actually, floorcloths are not easily compared with other types of floor coverings in terms of value or importance. Oilcloths, made in many qualities and weights for many purposes, included homemade types (often crude) which were plain but serviceable coverings for halls and other areas and richly decorated cloths for parlors and entrance halls. Beautiful professionally made cloths could be quite expensive, and it is evident that they were often used as status symbols. The versatility of the painted canvas was that it "could be adjusted in quality and design to fit the consumer's purse."[21]

Another factor in the popularity of oilcloth was its serviceability and durability, a factor that accounts for the current revival of its use in modern homes. An announcement in the *New Hampshire Gazette* of April 8, 1828, reads:

> *These carpets possess a decided advantage over all others, as they are more durable, and in warm weather much more comfortable, and easier to keep clean, and in hot climates the only kind that are not subject to injury from insects; in winter they may be covered with other carpeting without damage, and the room is kept warmer. . . ."*[22]

Eighteenth-century advertisements and inventories also provide clues to the variety of oilcloth types, widths, and uses. Cloths for heavy-traffic areas such as hallways and stairs were of more durable construction than those for rooms. References are made to "painted Oil Cloths" as well as "Fancy Pattern-Cloths." "Patent Oil Floor Cloths," available in a variety of standard widths,[23] were used wall-to-wall, as small rugs, and even on tables. Under a dining table, they were practical protection from stains.

5. Painted floorcloth (corner detail), eighteenth century. (Courtesy of The Henry Francis du Pont Winterthur Museum. catalog no. 61.1031.)

6. An accurate reproduction of the floorcloth from figure 5, according to the original specifications, created by Floorcloths, Inc., Annapolis, Maryland. A correctly made floorcloth of this type is extremely durable. See Technical Analysis section.

8. An accurate reproduction of
the floorcloth in figure 7
created by Floorcloths, Inc.,
Annapolis, Maryland. See
Technical Analysis section.

7. *Child with Dog*, American,
about 1800, oil. On the floor is
a simulated marble oilcloth.
(Courtesy of Abby Aldrich
Rockefeller Folk Art Collection, Williamsburg, Virginia.)

Floorcloths were used on bare floors, and at least by the early nineteenth century were sometimes placed under woven rugs in winter for warmth. In summer, they were preferred for coolness, alone or over a rug.[24]

Floorcloths and painted floors could be repaired and repainted—a thriving business in the eighteenth century and until the carpet industry spelled the decline of oilcloths in the 1830s and 1840s. In 1816, Samuel Perkins of Boston advertised "Old Carpets Repainted and Ornamented in the best manner."[25]

As mentioned, at first most designs—such as those of Mrs. John Adams[26]—imitated rugs, marble, parquet floors, or tile. An example of marbleized floor is shown in figures 7 and 8. This type of imitation continued, although some creativity developed in geometric and stylized floral and figurative patterns. American companies produced their own patterns. The free-hand designs that were initially prevalent were succeeded by stenciled and printed patterns with geometric layouts as illustrated in figures 9 and 10. The development of stenciling actually led to more intensive patterning.

Another remarkable example is a floorcloth at Melrose Plantation, Natchez, Mississippi, that imitates a Brussels carpet (figures 11 and 12). Inventories also mention cloths made to imitate Wilton and Brussels carpets.[27] Still others imitate ingrain. The stenciled floor reproduced at Bump Tavern in Cooperstown, New York, may have been inspired by an ingrain pattern.[28] Patterns imitating rugs often had ornamented borders, while diaper patterns might be without borders.

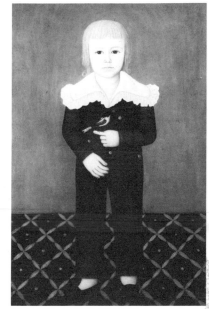

9. *Boy with Finch*, by John Brewster, Jr., about 1800, oil. Floor design is blue, orange, and yellow on a brown field. (Courtesy of the Abby Aldrich Rockefeller Folk Art Collection, Williamsburg, Virginia.)

10. *Nathan Hawley and Family* by William Wilkie, Albany, New York, 1801. Watercolor on paper. The floor of Sheriff Hawley's parlor is partly covered with a floorcloth painted with tan and blue motifs on a cream field. The floor in the back room is bare. (Courtesy of the Albany Institute of History and Art.)

11

11. Back hall of Melrose Plantation, Natchez, Mississippi, showing a painted floorcloth in imitation of a Brussels carpet. (Courtesy of Mrs. Dexter Ferry.)

12. Detail of fragment from the painted Brussels carpet imitation floorcloth shown in figure 11. Melrose Plantation also has a geometric floorcloth with marbleized effects in the front hall. (Courtesy of Mrs. Dexter Ferry.)

English firms produced pattern books of floor decorations as early as 1739, and they apparently influenced the American floorcloth-painting trade considerably (figure 4). The title page of one edition of John Carwitham's book of designs states:

> *Various kinds of FLOOR DECORATIONS represented both in Plano & Perspective Being useful Designs for Ornamenting the Floors of Halls Rooms, Summer Houses, &c. whither in Pavements of Stone, or Marble, or wth. Painted Floor Cloths, in Twenty four Copper Plates.*[29]

The floorcloth in figure 7 could have been derived from a Carwitham plate.

Some cloths were figurative, as demonstrated by account books of Reas and Johnston, Boston floorcloth painters. Among entries in the Daniel Reas firm is the following: "To Painting a Room and Entry Floor Cloath 35 yds. @ 2/8 with a Poosey-Cat on One Cloath and a Leetel Spannil on ye. Other Frenchman Like[£]4.13.4."[30] Most American firms of the period produced made-to-order cloths as well as cloths from their own designs.

The principal material in the ground for floorcloths is linen or cotton canvas in various weaves and weights. One such construction, for figure 6, is detailed later in the Technical

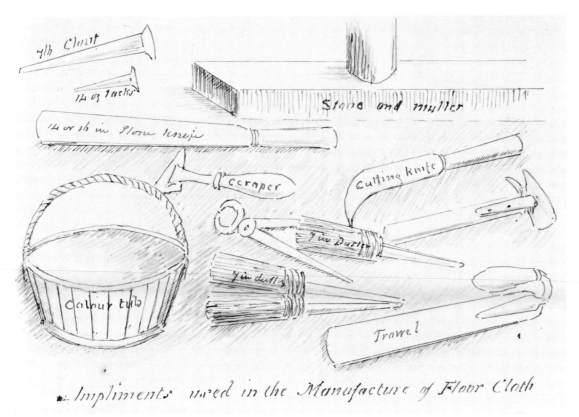

Impliments used in the Manufacture of Floor Cloth

Labels within image: 7lb Clout · 14 oz Tacks · 14 or 16 in Floor knife · Stone and muller · Scraper · Cutting knife · 7 in Duster · 7 in duster · Colour tub · Trowel

13. Eighteenth-century stenciling equipment for floorcloths used by Joseph Barnes of London, who also did house painting and produced block-printed cloths. (Courtesy of the Victoria and Albert Museum, London.)

Analysis section. The painting itself consists of many priming coats of oil paint, sanded and reprimed before the final coat—which may be plain or patterned—is applied. Little, who discusses the techniques in some detail, suggests at least five coats.[31] Some receipts for free-hand painting are more exotic though perhaps less chemically sound, such as this formula from *The Golden Cabinet*, Philadelphia, 1793.

> *The canvas being stretched on a frame give it a layer of size of paste water, then go over it with a pumice stone to smoothe off the knots. By means of the size the little threads and hairs are all laid close on the cloth, and the little holes filled up, so that no colour can pass through. When the cloth is dry lay on okre in oil which may be mixed with white lead to make it dry sooner. When dry go over again with pumice to make smoothe . . . . On this first draw the picture with a coal then lay on the colors. The use of a little honey mixed with the size will prevent cracking, peeling, and breaking out.*[32]

Proper drying of the layers of paint is critical to the process. Often the material, which is sometimes stretched, is hung in a large room with plenty of air circulation. Cloths may also have been laid out on the floor to dry. Varnish is often applied as a final protective coat. Cloths damaged by being rolled for shipment before they are thoroughly dry have been reported.[33] In 1767, Charles Carroll of Annapolis ordered oilcloths from England made well enough to "bear mopping over with a wet mop and Put up Dry and so as not to be Cracked or to have the Paint Rubbed of[f]."[34] It is well-known that water affects painted

13

14. Printed floorcloth, probably American, early nineteenth century. "The size of over-all printed design of this weft-twill cotton fabric indicates that, although rather light in weight, it was intended as a floorcloth. Since this example appears never to have been used it might be assumed that varnish or wax was to be applied to the surface after installation to provide body and greater durability as a floor covering." From Lanier, 1974, p. 40. Her caption contains technical data on the cloth. (Colonial Williamsburg photograph, no. G1952-15.)

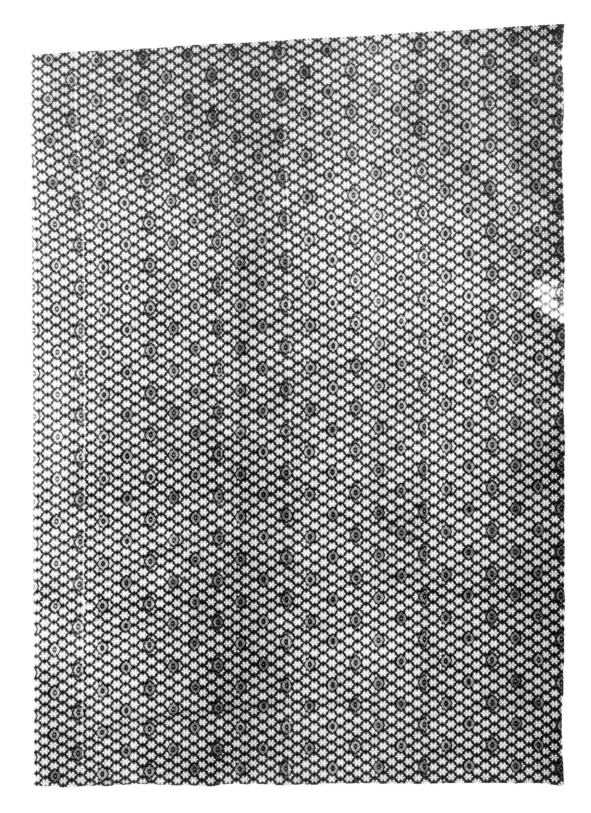

14

canvas adversely, but cloths were apparently washed — providing further need for their being well-made. Weather also affects the drying of oilcloths, hence the letter of David Spear, Jr., of Boston in 1767 to his fiancée stating that the carpet that his father is having painted for them "cannot be painted in the Winter Season, but in the Spring I hope to have it done."[35]

In eighteenth-century England stenciling gradually evolved as faster than other methods of decorating floorcloths, and Americans quickly followed suit. The equipment of Joseph Barnes of London, also a house painter, is illustrated in figure 13.

Stenciling was slightly more complex than free-hand painting. Rufus Porter, in *A Select Collection of Valuable and Curious Arts*, describes cutting out squares — pasteboard patterns which are laid on the floor or cloth and painted over.[36]

Block printing of floorcloths apparently began in about the mid-eighteenth century; Smith and Baber of London used its first block-printed pattern in 1754.

> *Fifteen-inch wooden printing blocks with looped leather hand-holds were pressed onto a paint cushion and then tapped smartly with a mallet to ensure a clean impression on the surface below.*[37]

For block printing, the surface was not necessarily primed beforehand. And after the pattern was printed the cloth could be varnished, shellacked, or waxed (figure 14).[38] Many old floorcloths such as those at Melrose (figures 11 and 12) show numerous coats of hardened, yellowed, and cracked varnish or shellac.

15. *The Medical Alchemist* by Viennese Franz Christoph Janneck, 1703-61. The table is covered with a woven or needlework cover. The Fisher Scientific Company collection of paintings on alchemy has numerous paintings with illustrations of rugs on tables, some of which are Turkish — particularly paintings by Justus Juncker (Dutch, 1703-67), Balthasar van den Bosch (Dutch, 1681-1715), and Jan Weiland (Rotterdam, b. 1861-?). (Courtesy of the Fisher Scientific Company, Pittsburgh, Pennsylvania.)

Oriental Rugs

L ittle is known about Oriental rugs in the West prior to the sixteenth century. The only evidence of their existence is their appearance in paintings, particularly during the Renaissance.[39] Most attempts to date early rugs are based on the study of these paintings. Rug patterns have been named after Renaissance artists, such as "Holbein carpets" or "Lotto carpets," even though these same patterns appear in the works of other artists. The first serious attempt to trace older Oriental rug history was made by Fredrik R. Martin in his book published in Vienna in 1908. The most important texts include those by Bode and Kühnel in 1958 and translations of two books by Erdmann in 1960 and 1970.

As noted in the section under "Sand and Straw," rugs were rare in Europe until late in its history. During the Renaissance, they were found mostly in the possession of nobility and in the churches. After long negotiations with the Venetian ambassador, Cardinal Wolsey had some Egyptian rugs imported into England in 1520 in exchange for diplomatic favors.[40] This was one of the first documented examples of Oriental rugs in England. Because they were so precious, rugs were not placed on the floor in the Oriental manner, but used on tables and on beds, as wall hangings, and as portières (figure 15).

Use of the term "rug" to denote a floor covering was not common in the West until the nineteenth century. The word comes from the old Norse *rögg* – meaning entangled hair — which led to the Norwegian *rugga* — meaning a coarse fabric. Any thick cover, blanket, or floor mat would qualify. Carpet, on the other hand, derives from the Latin *carpere*, referring to woolly clothes. In discussing Oriental rugs, the two terms have become interchangeable.[41] In English and industrial usage, however, distinctions are often made. Carpet refers to wall-to-wall coverings, one piece or seamed — often attached to the floor by tacking or other means. Very large rugs, even if not wall-to-wall, are sometimes also called carpets. Rugs, on the other hand, are restricted to smaller coverings of one piece and definite shape. In any case, *rug* may be used as the generic term.

Oriental rugs are mentioned in many American inventories, besides the romantic stories about Captain Kidd bringing in the first rug in 1700 as part of his booty. Although they were prized possessions in the eighteenth century — and even before[42] — not one single documented example has come down to us.[43] Our knowledge of types comes only from paintings, and only four American paintings depicting Oriental rugs were known until

17. *The Bermuda Group: Dean George Berkeley and His Family* by John Smibert, American, oil on canvas, 1729. The rug on the table is a "Transylvanian" design. (Courtesy of Yale University Art Gallery.) Another version of this painting, entitled *George Berkeley, Bishop of Cloyne, and his Wife and Family* by Smibert and dated 1729, is in the National Gallery of Ireland. There are conflicting scholarly opinions as to which is the earlier version.

OPPOSITE:

16. *Portrait of Elizabeth Franks*, attributed to Justus Englehardt Kuhn, oil, about 1708-10. The well-known "Lotto" design is shown in the rug. (Courtesy of the Milwaukee Art Center.)

18

recently when a fifth was uncovered; it is at the Milwaukee Art Center (figure 16). Two of the paintings show rugs on tables in the European manner; indeed, mention of rugs on the floor is rare before the mid-eighteenth century[44] (figures 17 and 18). Their rarity is further borne out by the infrequency with which new Oriental rugs were advertised in eighteenth-century newspapers. The trade was largely restricted to used rugs from estates and auctions.[45]

In 1765 Benjamin Franklin's wife asked him to get her a Turkey carpet while he was in London. He replied that he was shipping "A Large true Turkey Carpet cost 10 Guineas, for the Dining Parlour."[46] The fact that Franklin presumably had to acquire it in London points to the rarity and desirability of Oriental rugs. That Oriental rugs were a matter of prestige is clearly indicated by Copley's portrait of Jeremiah Lee and by Stuart's "Lansdowne" portrait of Washington (figures 19 and 20). Both gentlemen are standing on an Oriental rug. Many inventories of the second half of the eighteenth century show Oriental rugs, most of them huge, in the principal rooms of homes.[47]

Most Oriental rugs came to Europe and then to America by way of Turkey.[48] All of the rugs in the American paintings seem to be Turkish. Smyrna (now Izmir) was probably the port most frequently used, particularly for exporting the "Bergama" and "Uşak" designs of

18. *Isaac Royall and Family* by Robert Feke, American, 1741, oil. Compare the border with figures 22 and 23. (Courtesy of Harvard University, portrait collection, gift of Dr. George Stevens Jones.)

western Anatolia often seen in European paintings. This explains why rugs from Turkey are frequently called Smyrna carpets.

While few Persian rugs appear in early paintings, they were not entirely unknown in the eighteenth century. Writings distinguish between Turkish and Persian rugs. As early as 1579, an English spy was sent to Persia to investigate rug-dyeing secrets.[49]

In all probability, rugs from the Caucasus also traveled via Turkish ports. By the sixteenth century, rugs were being produced in Spain and Cairo, but there is no record of any of these in America in the eighteenth century.[50] Rugs from China and those made by central Asian nomads, including the so-called "Bokharas," were not imported, so that even if they were of the correct era they would not fit into an American period setting.[51]

The designs in the Smibert and Feke paintings show the "Transylvanian" type of rug (figures 17 and 18). There is some dispute among scholars as to whether these were made in Transylvania (Rumania), then controlled by the Ottomans, or in western Anatolia.[52] In any event, most were discovered in Transylvania churches. Good examples of these and other Turkish rugs of the period are at Colonial Williamsburg, The Metropolitan Museum in New York City,[53] and The Textile Museum in Washington, D.C. (figures 21-27).

The evolution of the rug loom runs the gamut from the portable ground loom used in ancient times by nomads in Central Asia — and still used as illustrated in figure 28 — to various types of upright looms found in villages and city factories of the Mideast as shown in

19. *Mr. Jeremiah Lee* by John Singleton Copley, 1769, oil painting. Col. Lee is standing on a Turkish rug which, according to McMullan (pages 221-222), "probably came through Smyrna." (Courtesy of Wadsworth Atheneum, Hartford, Connecticut.)

20. *George Washington*, "Landsdowne" portrait by Gilbert Stuart, 1795. The rug has a Uşak design. (Courtesy of the Pennsylvania Academy of Fine Arts.)

21. Caucasian "Dragon" rug, attributed to Kuba, eighteenth century. Rugs such as this may have come overland to the Black Sea or Smyrna for export to the West. A history and technical analysis may be found in Lanier (1975), plate 39. (Colonial Williamsburg photograph, no. 1963-198.)

23. "Transylvanian" rug. See Technical Analysis section. (Courtesy of The Textile Museum, Washington, D.C.; cat. no. R34.21.3.)

22. Border of a "Transylvanian" rug, taken from McMullan, 1965, (plate 86). Compare this border with the painting in figure 18. The original rug is now at the Metropolitan Museum of Art. (Drawing by Ruth Fisher.)

24. Rug from the Bergama district of Turkey, eighteenth–early nineteenth century. Similar rugs are still being made around Ezine. See Technical Analysis section. (Courtesy of The Textile Museum, Washington, D.C.; cat. no. R34.2.4.)

23

25. Uşak rug, Turkey, seventeenth – eighteenth century.
(Courtesy of The Textile
Museum, Washington, D.C.;
cat. no. R34.1.7.)

26. So-called "small patterned
Holbein," a Turkish rug type
frequently found in European
Renaissance paintings. (Cour-
tesy of The Textile Museum,
Washington, D.C.; cat. no.
R34.17.1.)

27. So-called "Lotto" pattern rug, named after a Turkish rug pattern found in Renaissance paintings of Lorenzo Lotto and others. A reproduction of this pattern was recently completed in Isparta, Turkey, for the St. John's Henrico Parish Church, Richmond, Virginia. (Courtesy of The Textile Museum, Washington, D.C.; cat. no. R34.18.2.)

28. Nomadic Lurs, camping near Khorramābād, Iran, weaving a rug on a ground loom. (Photograph by Léon A. Arkus, director, Museum of Art, Carnegie Institute, Pittsburgh. Taken during World War II.)

figure 29.[54] European tapestries also were often woven on similar looms.[55] As Europeans began to imitate Oriental rugs, they adapted upright tapestry looms. Horizontal treadle looms, also employed in France and England, were basic to homespun woven products in colonial America (figure 30).

Except for flat-woven rugs, the structure of most Oriental rugs was knotted pile, a form of extra-weft wrapping.[56] A number of "knots" were employed. The "Turkish" knot (such as "Gordes," "Chiordes," and "Symmetrical") was the most common in Anatolia, and with few exceptions was standard in English and American "Turkey work" (figure 31). Discussion of the terms used to describe this knot will be found in *Rugs Around the World* by Anthony Landreau and others scheduled for 1976 publication.

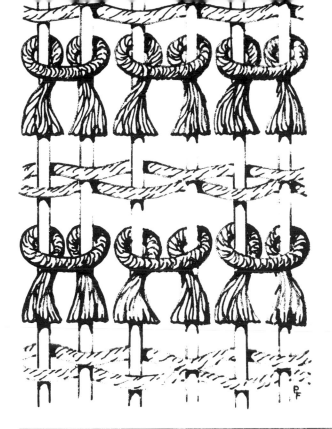

31. Diagram of the Turkish knot. (Drawing by Ruth Fisher.)

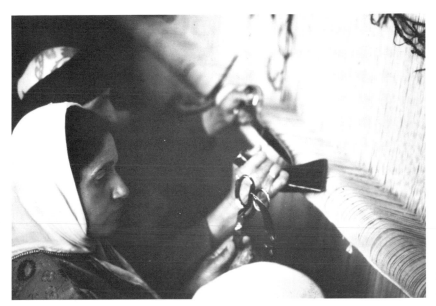

29. Weavers show their implements, beater and scissors, while seated at a typical upright loom as used in the villages of Persia and Asia Minor for centuries. (Photo by the author, Ören, Malatya District, Turkey, 1973.)

30. Weaver in attic using a treadle loom for producing rugs for the home. (Courtesy of Bigelow-Sanford, Inc.)

32. Turkey work upholstery
on a settee. Massachusetts,
about 1675. (Courtesy of the
Essex Institute, Salem.)

"Turkey Work" and the Axminster Carpet

After Oriental rugs were brought into Europe in the sixteenth century, there were many efforts to copy them. Spain developed its own rug-weaving culture and variant rug-making technique.[57] Folk-rug cultures developed in eastern Europe and elsewhere; throughout the period, Oriental designs were copied.[58] Oriental techniques were also used to produce local designs.

American inventories are not always clear as to whether Turkey carpets are actual Oriental examples or imitations. Turkish knots were used in English and American imitations, but the knots were usually less tightly packed than in Oriental rugs, often with a balanced knot count in warp and weft directions. Materials, however, differed. Linen and hemp warps were most common, as opposed to wool and cotton warps in the East. Silk was often used as a ground weft for the finer weaves.[59]

The "Turkey work" knotting technique was not restricted to rugs, but was also used for upholstery, chairs, stools, and the like. This type of work was popular in the sixteenth and seventeenth centuries, but diminished in the late seventeenth century when new styles of furniture came into vogue (figures 32-34).

By the beginning of the eighteenth century, production of "Turkey work" upholstery had come to a virtual standstill — needlework upholstery was preferred — however, some isolated examples from the early nineteenth century exist. At the same time, European production of rugs stopped because the European ones "could not compete with Oriental imports" which—thanks to "safe seas"—were becoming more plentiful and less expensive.[60]

Hand-knotted rugs were revived in England in 1750 when weavers from the Savonnerie factory in France opened a shop in Westminster. This venture failed, but it gave impetus to Thomas Whitty of Axminster and others to start rug factories using the Turkish knot. Axminster rugs gained fame, and the name was applied to all such products.[61] A type of weave produced by modern machines still bears the Axminster name (figure 79). Production of true Axminster types declined in the 1820s, however, with the development of the machine carpet industry. In 1835 the Axminster operations were transferred to Wilton, where they were continued on a small scale. Both Oriental and Axminster types declined at about the same time and both were revived in the 1870s — Orientals because of renewed

33. Turkey work upholstery on chair. England, late seventeenth century. For historical and technical analysis of this piece see Lanier, 1975, p. 8. (Courtesy of Colonial Williamsburg, photograph no. 1936-168.)

35. *The Samels Family* by Johann Eckstein, American, 1788, oil. The rug is suggestive of floral Axminsters of the period. (Courtesy of the Museum of Fine Arts, Boston. Ellen Kelleran Gardner Fund. 59.19.)

34. Fragments of Turkey work chair upholstery. England, seventeenth century. For historical and technical analysis of this piece see Lanier, 1975, p. 6. (Courtesy of Colonial Williamsburg, photograph no. 1954-375.)

interest in them as art, and Axminsters largely through the effort of William Morris who started a factory for hand-knotting in 1878.[62]

English Axminsters were imported into the United States such as are shown in figures 35 and 36. Some hand-knotted rugs were also made here. William P. Sprague was operating a hand-knotting shop in Philadelphia in 1791.[63] A well-known "Turkey" rug, homemade by Ann and Parnell Nevill in 1746 in England, was eventually brought to the United States and is exhibited at Mount Vernon (figure 37). Other examples of Axminster types are at Winterthur, Colonial Williamsburg, and elsewhere.

30

36. Knotted carpet, English, possibly Axminster, late eighteenth century. For historical and technical analysis of this piece see Lanier, 1975, p. 26. (Courtesy of Colonial Williamsburg, photograph no. 1956-178.)

37. Knotted rug signed by Ann and Parnell Nevill, 1746, made in England, now at Mount Vernon. (Courtesy of the Mount Vernon Ladies' Association of the Union.)

38. Needlework rug, English,
1740-65.) For historical and
technical analysis of this piece
see Lanier, 1975, p. 16.
(Courtesy of Colonial Williamsburg, photograph no.
1956-649.)

Folk Rugs

In the early eighteenth century, needlework replaced Turkey work for upholstery. And needlework rugs, intended for use on the floor, also became popular in eighteenth-century England. The most common stitches were the tent-stitch and the cross-stitch, done in wool on linen canvas.[64] Designs tended toward either imitations of Oriental rugs or exotic floral creations (figure 38). Needlework carpets continued to be produced in the nineteenth century (figure 39). There is little evidence of their being made or used in eighteenth-century America although there was at least one in 1790.[65] The earliest existing American example (1810-12) may be in The Metropolitan Museum of Art; it is from the home of Judge Pliny Moore of Champlain, New York.[66]

There is no mention of tapestry-woven rugs made or used in America. Colonial Williamsburg has an eighteenth-century cotton, tapestry-woven floorcloth which was probably woven in England. (figure 40). Although kilims, tapestry-woven rugs of the Middle East, were not popular as collectors' items until recent times,[67] they were imported in large quantities after the revival period (1870s) for such uses as portières and upholstery.[68] Many must have come to the West in earlier times also, but it is not known if any were used on the floor; no records or examples remain. The same might apply to the European tapestry rugs, particularly those produced in France. Although they were almost as accessible to colonists as English rugs, there seems to be no record of their use. Less durable than pile rugs, tapestry rugs may have been less desirable for floor coverings.

In the second half of the nineteenth century, the practice began of using rugs native to America on the floors of American homes. These were the rugs made by Indians in the southwestern United States, particularly the Navaho. The Navaho originally wove their rugs as articles of dress — "blankets" — a usage that still justifies their being called rugs according to the meaning of the term set forth under our heading, "Oriental Rugs." Their use on the floor was precipitated by the settlers. From 1890 to 1900, the Navaho weaving industry "had long since changed from the weaving of wearing apparel to an article best described as a coarse rug."[69] The modern revival of Navaho weaving has centered on rugs and wall hangings with designs, materials, and dyes of a quality that is better than ever (figure 41).

Perhaps the earliest type of homemade carpeting was the plain-weave striped rug (figure 42). A Williamsburg inventory of 1749 mentions a list carpet.[70] The homemade rugs could

39. Needlework rug, English, nineteenth century. For historical and technical analysis of this piece see Lanier, 1975, p. 22. (Courtesy of Colonial Williamsburg, photograph no. 1956-45.)

40. Tapestry-woven floorcloth, probably English, eighteenth century. For historical and technical analysis of this piece see Lanier, 1975, p. 42. (Courtesy of Colonial Williamsburg, photograph no. 1956-537.)

34

42. *The Talcott Family* by Deborah Goldsmith, New York, 1832, watercolor. Note the homemade striped carpet on the floor. (Courtesy of the Abby Aldrich Rockefeller Folk Art Collection, Williamsburg, Virginia.)

41. Twentieth-century Navaho rug. See Technical Analysis section. (Courtesy of Section of Man, Museum of Natural History, Carnegie Institute, Pittsburgh.)

35

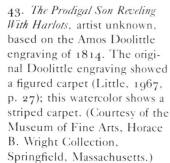

be all wool, wool warp with cotton weft, cotton warp with tow-flax weft, or other variations.[71] They could be warp- or weft-faced. Ordinarily, they were woven strips sewn together and were used as rugs and for wall-to-wall carpeting. Striped rugs of this type appear in English and Dutch paintings[72] and, like straw mats and baize, have sometimes been used as covers for pile rugs (figure 44). The cheapest and most easily woven was the list, or rag, rug: strips of woven wool, cotton, or linen were sewn together and inserted as weft. Rag rugs of this type are still produced in Appalachia (figure 45).

Although the origin of "Venetian" carpeting has not been satisfactorily traced, it does not appear to bear any relationship to Venice.[73] The carpeting, usually for halls and stairs, might be described as cheap material with striped woolen or worsted warps which cover the wefts. Venetian carpeting, first used in the early nineteenth century, may have been originally produced in small hand factories, but then certainly became part of the early industrial development in the United States (figures 46 and 47). The structure of Venetian carpeting changed in the industrial era[74] to that of a 2-ply fabric with cotton or wool warp and wool filler; later jute was used as the filler. "It differed from the two-ply ingrain in that the warp threads were colored and that they, not the filling yarns, produced the figure in the article."[75] Made of coarse wool or even wool-hair mixtures, Venetians never approached the

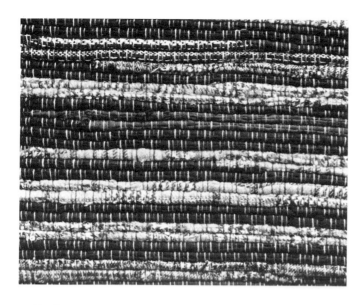

45. Detail of modern "rag rug" made by Silvia Spradlin of the Paint Creek Weavers in Paint Creek, Kentucky, 1975. The structure is traditional, even though quality and design are altered. See Technical Analysis section. (Photograph by Elton Schnellbacher.)

46. Venetian carpeting fragment, nineteenth century. See Technical Analysis section. (Courtesy of the Division of Textiles, National Museum of History and Technology, Smithsonian Institution, no. T.4908.)

47. Detail of "Venetian" carpeting, American, nineteenth century. (Courtesy of Colonial Williamsburg, photograph no. G1967-721.

49. Old braided rug, utilizing many fabrics. See Little, 1967, figures 32-33. (Courtesy of Old Sturbridge Village, Massachusetts.)

48. "Venetian" carpeting, leather-trimmed mail sack, American, early nineteenth century. The durable Venetian carpeting was also used for mail pouches such as this one used on the Rochester–Canandaigua, New York, route opened in 1815 (Roth, p. 48). (Courtesy of the Rochester Historical Society.)

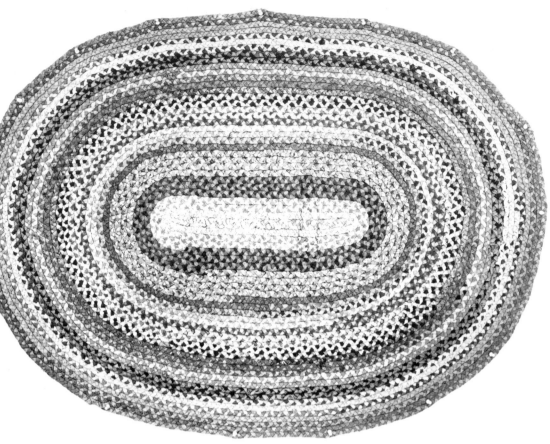

50. Detail of rug in figure 49. The technique is three-strand braiding.

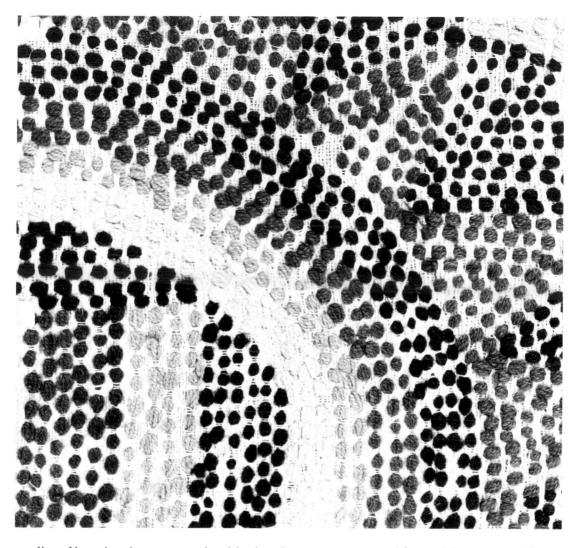

52. Detail of back of figure 51, showing separate stitches on the linen ground. Shives from the coarse linen ground are evident.

quality of ingrains, but were so durable that they were even used for such items as mailbags. (figure 48).

Hooked, braided, and other types of homemade rugs may have been made in the late eighteenth century, but there is little evidence. They are, therefore, inappropriate for eighteenth-century settings. A patchwork rug is mentioned in 1802.[76] It is not known when braided rag rugs were first used, but their history is traceable from the early nineteenth century, when they were common, to the present (figures 49 and 50).

The sewn rug is perhaps the best known homemade type. There are three main categories[77] and many variations. Yarn-sewn rugs, some with designs going back to the 1780s, are probably the earliest (figure 51). They were flexible and were used both as bed and floor rugs. The woolen design yarn was sewn through the linen ground canvas in a series of short stitches.[78] Such rugs are easily identified by the separate stitches on the back (figure 52).

Shirred rugs constitute the second general type. Most of these appeared between 1825

51. Yarn-sewn rug, wool on linen, late eighteenth–early nineteenth century. Illustrated in Little, 1967, figure 35. (Courtesy of Old Sturbridge Village, Massachusetts.)

39

53. Shirred rug. Woolen cloth sewn to linen ground. Unlike yarn-sewn rugs, the material will not show on the back, only the stitches used to secure it. Illustrated in Little, 1967, figure 39. (Courtesy of Old Sturbridge Village, Massachusetts.)

and 1860. Strips of felt or printed dress material were shirred—gathered—with a needle and sewn to the canvas surface. The needle stitches, but no design yarn, show on the back side[79] (figures 53 and 54).

Hooked rugs, proper, are made by drawing the fabric strips "with a hook from back to front, in the same aperture, through a coarse foundation. The strips remain looped on the surface, but are carried along flat on the under side to be pulled through again to form the next loop . . . [resulting] in continuous rows of flat stitches on the reverse, with no open spaces between such as appear in a yarn-sewn rug."[80] Hooking probably began later than yarn-sewn and shirred rugs and is still done in Shaker communities and in other isolated areas (figures 55 and 56). A burlap foundation indicates that the rug was made after the mid-nineteenth century because jute, used in burlap, was not imported earlier.[81] Nina Fletcher Little in her book on *Floor Coverings in New England before 1850* illustrates one (undated) hooked rug in the design of a Turkish rug.[82] Modern hooking and needlework kits also often provide quasi-Oriental rug patterns.

40

54. Shirred rag rug with braided edge, predominant colors rust-brown, pink, olive, black, and greys in the Centre Family House Museum. (Courtesy of Shakertown at Pleasant Hill, Harrodsburg, Kentucky.)

55. Hooked rug with braided rag border. White horse on green background, four red hearts; border of red, light blue, navy, and off-white. Another hooked horse rug, nineteenth century, from Pleasant Hill is illustrated in Christensen, plate 38. (Centre Family House Museum. Courtesy of Shakertown at Pleasant Hill, Harrodsburg, Kentucky.)

56. Hooked rug with leopard design, wool on linen, about 1820. Another Shelburne hooked rug is illustrated in Lipman-Winchester, p. 278. (Courtesy of Shelburne Museum, Shelburne, Vermont.)

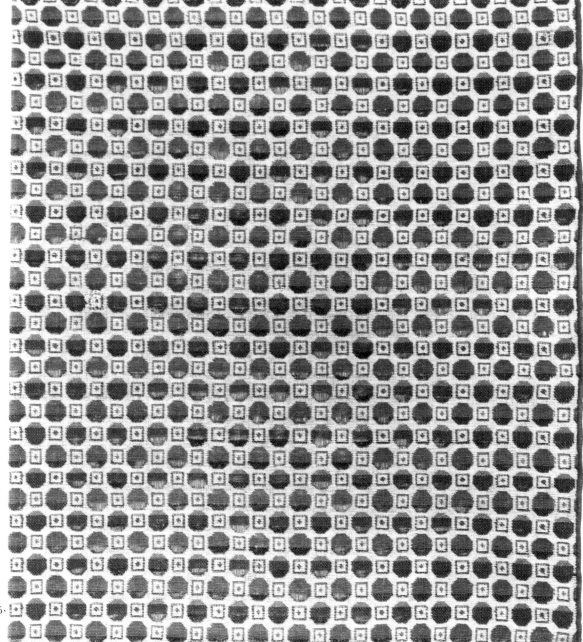

58. Scotch carpeting, eighteenth–nineteenth century. Worsted double-cloth. The small repeat pattern designs were more durable for double-cloth. Parquet and mosaic patterns were often used. For historical and technical analysis see Lanier, 1975, p. 38. (Courtesy of Colonial Williamsburg, photograph no. G1956-297.)

The Great American Carpet Industry

The American carpet industry became powerful in the early nineteenth century and since 1840 has dominated the world carpet industry. Dominated by one man, Erastus B. Bigelow, it traces the industry from a few hand shops to a giant factory system. It is a Horatio Alger story of American initiative and inventive genius. The American success story, but surprisingly devoid of the labor abuse and agitation that plagued other emerging industries of the era.[83]

Ingrains

The early history revolves about a type known as ingrain, which dominated carpet production throughout the nineteenth century. According to Arthur Cole and Harold Williamson,[84] the name derives from the design "ingrained in the web of the fabric," created by interweaving warp and weft. Mildred Lanier suggests,[85] however, that the term possibly derived from the fact that the worsted warp — the "chain" — and the worsted or woolen wefts "were dyed 'in grain' meaning in the yarn or in the fiber" — that is, prior to manufacture. Neither definition is particularly accurate, because either could apply to many different types of weaves. Technically, most ingrains are double, or triple, cloth carpeting which is reversible. Compound weaves other than double and triple cloth were also woven.[86]

The double-cloth variety was first made in Kidderminster, England, about 1735 and was also woven in Kilmarnock, Scotland, about 1780. Most handmade British carpets of this type, and eventually other types as well, became known as Scotch carpets (figures 57 and 58); however, the terms ingrain, Kidderminster, Kilmarnock, Scotch, English, and even Irish have been applied interchangeably to double-cloth carpeting. The descriptively accurate terms, "double-cloth" or "triple-cloth carpeting," would be more appropriate. Throughout their history, ingrains have been regarded as relatively cheap although the advent of 3-ply weaves improved their quality. Usually woven in narrow widths—about 36 inches—ingrains were often used for halls and stairs or sewn together for room carpeting.

George Conradt, who came to Frederick, Maryland, from Württemberg in the "early 19th century," may have woven the first ingrains in the United States, according to a book published by the Bigelow-Hartford Carpet Company in 1925. Ingrained as well as plain

57. Scotch carpeting, eighteenth–nineteenth century. Worsted double-cloth woven ingrain was sometimes used for other purposes such as here for a horse blanket and for carpet bags. This blanket has a quilted cotton lining and a worsted tape trim, leather and brass fastenings, worn condition. (Courtesy of Colonial Wiliamsburg, photograph no. 1968-7; For history, see Lanier, 1975, p. 36).

43

60. *Girl Coming Through Doorway* by George Washington Mark, Greenfield, Massachusetts, 1875, oil. Probably an ingrain carpet is represented on the floor, although it could be a painted imitation. (Courtesy of Greenfield Village and Henry Ford Museum, Dearborn, Michigan.)

59. *Colonel Benjamin Tallmadge and His Son, William,* by Ralph Earl, 1790, oil painting. "The patterned floor covering of this room extends to the walls where it is edged with a harmonious border. This distinguished citizen of Connecticut, a Member of Congress from 1801 to 1817, and president of a bank in Litchfield, is depicted in a domestic setting with books, fringe-decorated chair and table cover, and vivid-figured floor covering." (Roth, p. 34, figure 16.) (Courtesy of Litchfield Historical Society.)

61. Ingrain carpet, about 1840, on the floor of the Ladies' Parlor at Bump Tavern, The Farmers' Museum, Cooperstown, New York. (Courtesy of New York State Historical Association.)

striped carpets were probably woven in eighteenth-century America: inventories and advertisements mention great quantities of imported double-cloth carpeting in America in the eighteenth century[87] (figures 59 and 60). By the end of the century, there were small workshops in Philadelphia where carpets were woven. The "rug manufacturing shop" opened there by William Calverly in 1775 is claimed to be the earliest in America.[88] We have seen that William Sprague was making Turkey rugs in Philadelphia, and Peter Stowell had a small workshop in Worcester, Massachusetts, in 1794. In the North, rugmaking was primarily a household activity in the eighteenth century, while in the Philadelphia area there was a "putting out" system whereby work was farmed out to home weavers. A similar system still exists in some areas of Turkey and Persia. From this, the small shop system evolved: even after the inauguration of the New England industry, Philadelphia manufacture tended to remain small and devoted to the cheaper 2-ply carpets.

The early story of power-loom carpet weaving in the United States is in essence the story of the fertile brain and ceaseless energy of Erastus Bigelow. He, almost single-handedly, is responsible for most of the important early inventions relating to the carpet industry in America, and his basic devices were still essentially intact and in use one hundred years later.[89] A coach-lace loom that Bigelow invented embodied the principles of his later carpet looms. By 1842 he had patented his ingrain power loom, which was operating successfully at the Lowell Carpet Company in 1843 (figures 62-64). Subsequent improvements, especially his 1846 Jacquard power loom for Brussels carpeting, and the development of

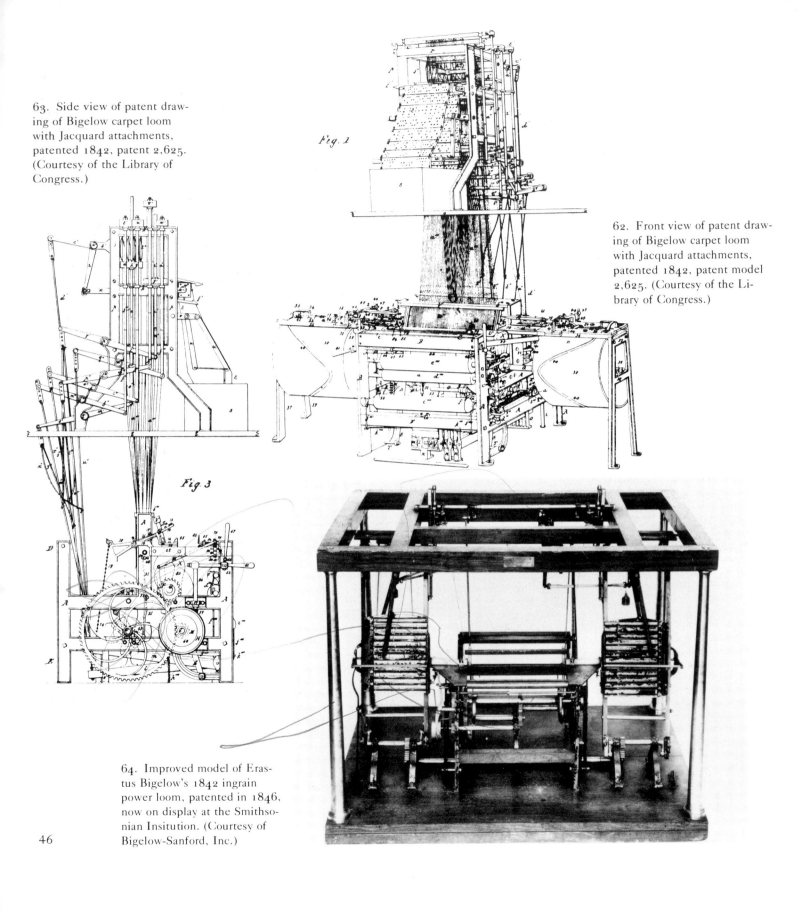

63. Side view of patent drawing of Bigelow carpet loom with Jacquard attachments, patented 1842, patent 2,625. (Courtesy of the Library of Congress.)

Fig. 1

62. Front view of patent drawing of Bigelow carpet loom with Jacquard attachments, patented 1842, patent model 2,625. (Courtesy of the Library of Congress.)

Fig. 3

64. Improved model of Erastus Bigelow's 1842 ingrain power loom, patented in 1846, now on display at the Smithsonian Insitution. (Courtesy of Bigelow-Sanford, Inc.)

multiple-shuttle boxes for wefting eventually led to mass production not only of 2- and 3-ply ingrains, but many other weaves.

Most factory-made rugs were ingrain carpeting in the early period and even by 1899 comprised more than 50 percent of total production.[90] Many designs were patented (figures 65-70). By about 1833, 3-ply (triple-cloth) ingrains with gaudy floral designs were replacing the cheaper 2-ply (figures 71 and 72). C. R. Fish, *In the Rise of the Common Man: 1830-1850*, puts it graphically:

> *A Cult of nature arose, a strange conventionalized or sentimentalized nature remote from reality. The gorgeous flora of carpets was perhaps its worst expression.*[91]

65. Two-ply (double-cloth) handwoven ingrain carpeting, Jacquard patterning of floral and geometric designs in red, greens, black, and yellow, dated 1884. See Technical Analysis section. (Courtesy of the Smithsonian Institution, Division of Textiles, no. T.7429.)

66. Two-ply (double-cloth) in-grain carpeting, probably used in New England (purchased in Stamford, Connecticut) mid-nineteenth century, alternating sections of brown and white, green and red. See Technical Analysis section. (Courtesy of the Smithsonian Institution, Division of Textiles no. T.16934.)

67. Two-ply (double-cloth) in-grain carpeting in leaf design, red, black, yellow, white, pale green, golden brown. Woven by Lowell Carpet Company in 1884. See Technical Analysis section. (Courtesy of the Smithsonian Institution, Division of Textiles, no. T.7419.)

68. Two-ply (double-cloth) ingrain carpeting, patented by
W. Wallace, June 14, 1870,
patent 104,232. This type
sometimes is referred to as
"damask carpet." The foliage
design is black, red, yellow,
white. See Technical Analysis
section. (Courtesy of the
Smithsonian Institution, Division of Textiles, no. T. 11395.)

69. Two-ply (double-cloth) ingrain carpeting with so-called "damask" border (see Emery, 1966, pp. 133-136); red and grey center pattern; borders of white, brown, green, yellow, red, and orange. Patented by John Dorman Carpets, September 9, 1873, Patent 142,681. See Technical Analysis section. (Courtesy of the Smithsonian Institution, Division of Textiles, no. T.11395.)

70. Two-ply (double-cloth) ingrain carpeting woven to look like Brussels carpeting, floral design, green and brown ground with white, light blue, and gold. Patented by T. B. Dorman, Dec. 9, 1896, Patent 574,023. See Technical Analysis section. (Courtesy of the Smithsonian Institution, Division of Textiles, no. T.11395.)

71. Three-ply (triple-cloth) ingrain carpeting, floral design no. 856, Lowell Carpeting Company, 1884. Red, brown, white, green. See Technical Analysis section. (Courtesy of the Smithsonian Institution, Division of Textiles, no. T.7415.)

72. Three-ply (triple-cloth)
ingrain carpeting. Bigelow-
Sanford, nineteenth century
(undated). See Technical
Analysis section. (Courtesy of
the Smithsonian Institution,
Division of Textiles, no.
T.11448.)

Brussels, Wiltons, and Other Commercial Carpets

Brussels carpeting dates to Flemish supremacy in the arts.[92] In 1740, England's first Brussels carpet factory in England was begun at Wilton. Brussels carpets were also made at Kidderminster starting about 1749. They were imported into America from England after 1750 and, while not so popular as Wiltons, are mentioned in many contemporary inventories and advertisements.[93] President John Adams had Brussels carpeting at the White House. In 1807, Isaac Macaulay bought the oilcloth factory of John Dorsey—established that year in Philadelphia—and began weaving Brussels carpets in what was probably the first carpet factory in the United States.[94]

The principle of the Brussels carpet is that, as required by the design, warps supplementary to the ground warps are passed over a rod. When the rod is removed, the warps form a pile loop above the surface of the fabric, which is held by ground wefts beaten into place between rows of loops. Pile fabrics in this technique have been found in ancient Egypt (figure 73).

Wiltons are woven in essentially the same way. At Wilton, the pile loops were cut to provide a more velvety surface and more precise design (figure 74). Cut-loop rugs came to be called Wiltons. Apparently this technique had also been used in Flanders for high-

73. Diagram of the construction of a Brussels carpet. (Drawing by Ruth Fisher.)

74. Diagram of the construction of a Wilton carpet. (Drawing by Ruth Fisher.)

54

75. Carpet, said to be hand-made Wilton-type, about 1750 (Little, p. 8, figure 5). Brought from England where it was a cut from a carpet at Ramsbury Manor, Wiltshire, it is presently in the governor's bedroom at Tryon. This carpet imitates a Persian design and is typical of the type of Wilton found in America at that period. (Courtesy of Tryon Place Restoration, New Bern, North Carolina.)

quality carpets and had been well known in ancient times: it is found in the velvets of the Han Dynasty in China and in Safawid Persia.

Wiltons were popular (figure 75). George Washington ordered one for Mount Vernon.[95] They may have been considered by some as the ultimate in floor coverings in the early nineteenth century, as expressed by John Quincy Adams.

> *And maples, of fair glossy stain,*
> *Must form my chamber doors,*
> *And carpets of the Wilton grain*
> *Must cover all my floors.*[96]

Prior to the industrial era most Brussels and Wilton carpets were made in narrow widths and had to be sewn together for room carpeting.

Production of Wilton and Brussels carpeting was limited in the early industrial period but gained impetus with the development of the Bigelow Brussels-Wilton loom in 1849. The machines for Wilton differed only in that they had a device to cut the pile (figure 76).[97] Wiltons are still produced. Since the structure for both Wilton and Brussels carpets is the same, both are often called Wilton (figures 77 and 78).

The development of the so-called "tapestry" and velvet carpets was intimately tied to the

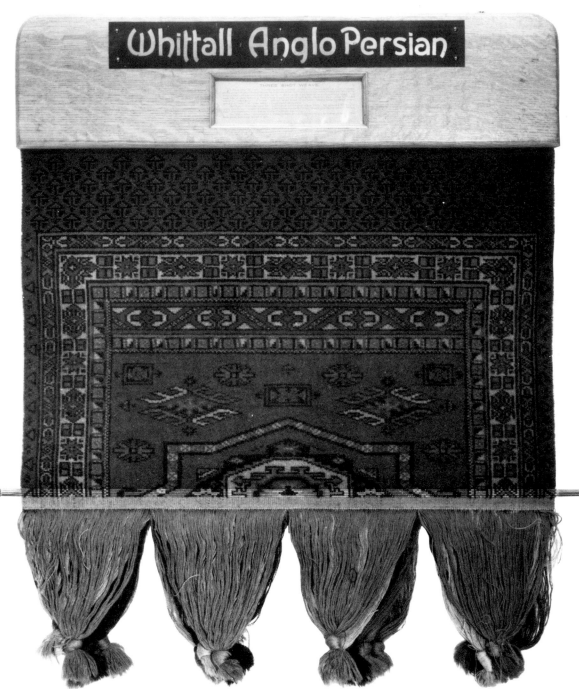

76. "Whittall Anglo-Persian" Wilton sampler with weaving rods in place, undated. The legend says in part: ". . . the 'weft' is carried through the fabric three times to every row of tufts . . . while in a 2 shot weave it crosses but twice, giving it only a double binding which is not sufficient for a tufted worsted carpet. . . . The '3 shot' is the only weave that 'locks' firmly the . . . 'tufts' that make up a Wilton . . . there being over (18,000) . . . 'tufts' in each square foot of our Anglo Persian rugs . . . The '3 shot weave' is not essential in a Brussels fabric, since there are no 'tufts'; the worsted yarns on the face being uncut, form loops instead of tufts." (Courtesy of Merrimack Valley Textile Museum, North Andover, Massachusetts, cat. no. 64.46. See Technical Analysis section.)

56

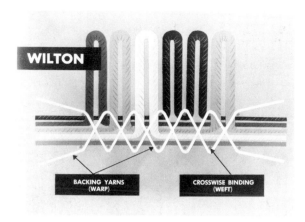

WILTON

BACKING YARNS (WARP) CROSSWISE BINDING (WEFT)

77. Diagram of a modern Wilton or Brussels carpet. Since the structure is the same for both types, they are often called Wilton in the industry. (Courtesy of the Carpet and Rug Institute, Dalton, Georgia.)

78. Brussels carpet, dated 1884. Gift of Bigelow-Sanford. See Technical Analysis section. (Courtesy of the Smithsonian Institution, Division of Textiles, no. 7399.)

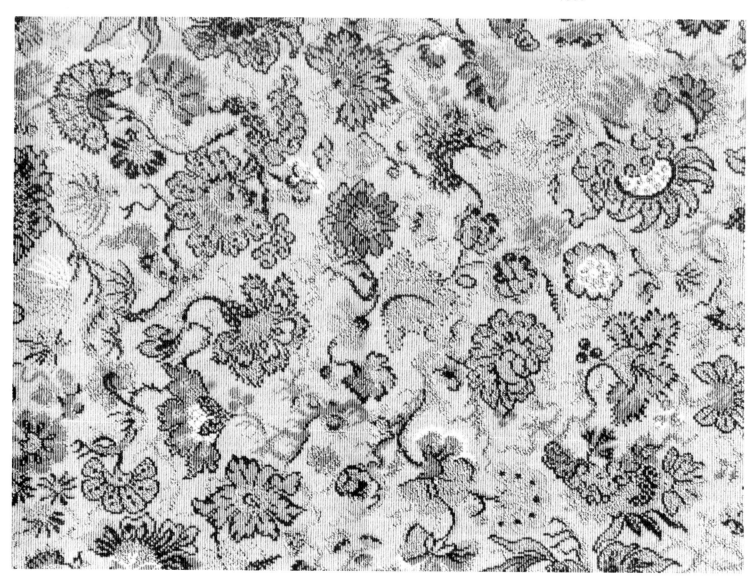

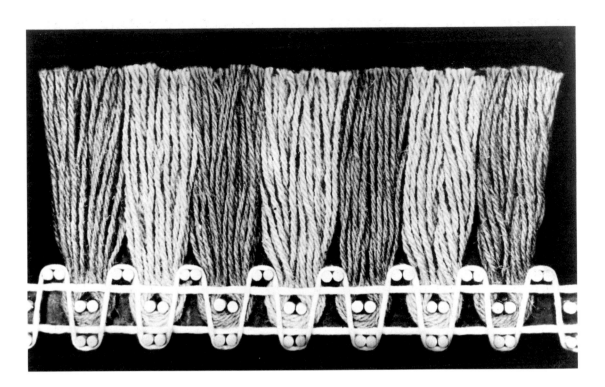

79. Diagram of modern "Axminster" weave. (Courtesy of the Carpet and Rug Institute, Dalton, Georgia.)

development of the printing drum by Richard Whytock of Edinburgh in 1832. "Tapestry" in this case has nothing to do with the structure known as tapestry,[98] nor does the word "velvet" describe structure. These techniques were evolved to find a cheaper way of producing Wilton and Brussels carpets. Instead of the multiframe loom, only

> *a single set of wool yarns . . . supplies the place of the four or five sets of yarns (or 'frames') required by the more elegant Brussels and Wilton . . . the yarns are not dyed a single color, but each strand of yarn is given a series of colors at intervals along its length which correspond to the color-pattern demanded for that yarn in the makeup of the woven fabric.*[99]

The only difference between "tapestry" and "velvet" is that "velvet" has cut looped pile similar to Wiltons. Other variations of these techniques have evolved.

Several factors influenced the final great nineteenth-century development in power machinery, the "Axminster" loom. Devised between 1856 and 1874, it is credited to the genius of Halcyon Skinner and Alexander Smith.[100] The importation of jute into the United States in the 1850s had led to a filler which was cheaper than wool for rugs and had become essential to the future of the industry. In addition, manufacturers sought to save pile wool by not burying it in the body and at the back of the fabric, while at the same time seeking ways to provide more colors and a wider variety of designs. Axminster was the answer to these needs and helped to revolutionize the industry at that time.

The result bore no structural relationship to the original Axminsters although the appearance approximated it. Many types of "Axminster" systems and improvements have been developed over the years, but the basic idea involves a separate spool of yarn for each

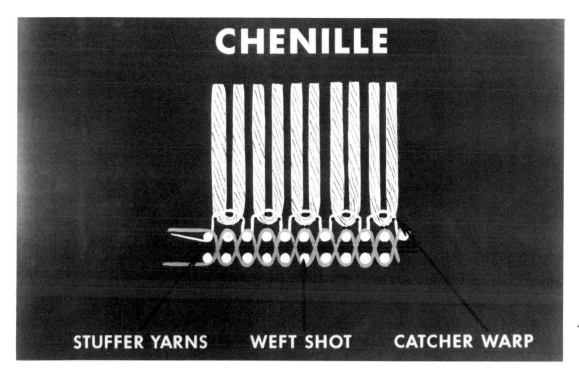

CHENILLE

STUFFER YARNS   WEFT SHOT   CATCHER WARP

80. Diagram of a modern "chenille" weave. (Courtesy of the Carpet and Rug Institute, Dalton, Georgia.)

row in the design dyed with appropriate colors for each tuft of pile. The spools are arranged above the loom in an endless chain in the correct order, and the yarn is inserted and cut off for each tuft in the row of weaving. Weft threads are shot across to hold the pile in place (figure 79).

Another type of carpet developed during the formative years of the carpet industry was chenille. The name comes from the French word for caterpillar and refers to tufted cord. Chenille carpets are made by first weaving a weft pile and cutting it into strips. This "fur" is then set into a backing of jute and cotton yarns (figure 80). The so-called Smyrna carpeting of the 1870s was a two-faced version of the chenille weave.[101] "Smyrna" in this case is an industrial term, and has nothing to do with the handmade Turkish rugs imported through Smyrna in the eighteenth and nineteenth centuries.

81. Candlewick bedspread made by Catherine Evans Whitener (1883-1963) of Dalton, Georgia. (Courtesy of the Carpet and Rug Institute, Dalton, Georgia.)

The Second Revolution: The Tufted Carpet and Other Modern Innovations

There are basically three types of industrial carpets: woven, sewn (tufted), and knitted. Until 1950, almost all industrial carpeting was woven. Many variations of ingrain, Axminster, Brussels, Wilton, tapestry types, and chenille evolved after 1825. By 1900, broadloomed carpet was in use. The innovations continued until World War II. It may be surprising to note that none of these weaving techniques except Wilton and Axminster is still used in the United States. Wiltons and Axminsters are only made on a very limited scale.[102] The era of the woven rug has been rapidly eclipsed.

In the 1950s, there was a revolution in carpetmaking as tremendous in its impact as the original industrial revolution and the inventions of Erastus Bigelow. It could be called the tufted revolution. From humble beginnings in Dalton, Georgia, the tufting industry has risen to completely dominate the field of carpetmaking.

Colonial Americans had decorated bedspreads by saving candlewicks and inserting them as tufts. And in 1895 home industry was inadvertently begun by a teenager, Catherine Evans Whitener, who copied an antique candlewick spread (figure 81). The sale of one of her products for $2.50 in 1900 led to the development of a great industry. By the 1920s there was a large handmade tufted-bedspread industry in Dalton, Georgia. Single-needle tufting machines were introduced to increase production. By 1940, Joe Cobble had invented a multineedle machine which tufted across the whole width of the bedspread.

Before 1949, few carpets were made this way. A bath-mat industry had evolved from the 1920s. Latexing was first used to make the mats skidproof and hold the pile to the backing. Production of carpeting began in earnest in 1949. Dalton became the capital of the industry, and the move to the South began. By 1965 more than 85 percent of the carpet production in the United States was tufted. Our nation reasserted its leadership role in carpetmaking. Today, almost all machine-made carpeting is tufted. Innovations and inventions are being tried all the time, but the story of the modern "revolution through evolution" is due primarily to the development of the tufting process—in which pile yarns are inserted with needles into a previously woven fabric. In other words, "a modern tufting machine may be considered as a giant sewing machine having hundreds of needles."[103] See figures 82 and 83. Tufted carpeting may be made in both cut and uncut pile. At first it was in a single color, but gradually multicolored tufting was developed.

The first step into modern tufting came in 1949 when Cabin Crafts (now part of West

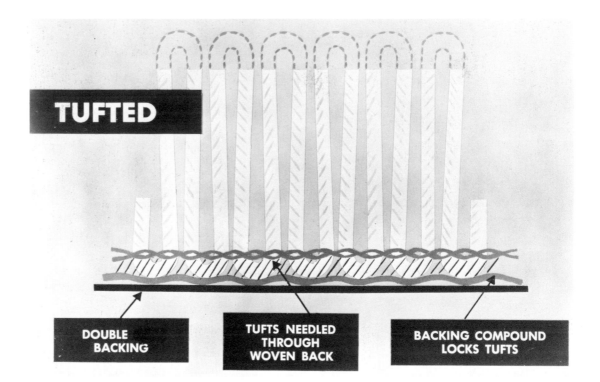

TUFTED

| DOUBLE BACKING | TUFTS NEEDLED THROUGH WOVEN BACK | BACKING COMPOUND LOCKS TUFTS |

82. Diagram of a modern tufted carpet construction. (Courtesy of the Carpet and Rug Institute, Dalton, Georgia.)

Point Pepperell, Inc.) began tufting wide broadloom under the leadership of Fred Westcott, founder and first president. Previously, most woven and tufted carpet had been produced in 27-inch widths, which were seamed together later. Today, it is woven up to 15 feet wide.

Today's tufted carpet has four basic parts: the yarns inserted into the preformed backing; the backing itself, known as primary back; the latex spread on the back of the carpet, mainly to bind the tufts into place to add stability; and a secondary back applied after tufting.

Many types of backing have been tried, including domestic sheeting.

In the early 1950s wide looms were developed, and jute — cheap and strong — was woven into backing fiber. Jute is still used, but in the last decade synthetics have dominated as primary backing. Travis Rhodes of Dalton, Georgia—working with James Lees and Sons Company—patented a successful commercial synthetic backing fabric for the carpet industry in the early 1960. This major breakthrough enabled the industry to continue to grow rapidly without depending upon an unstable foreign supply.

In 1957, Cabin Crafts and Patchogue Plymouth Company introduced a second backing. Laminated to the tufted carpet, it provided the stability, strength, and performance needed for wall-to-wall installations. It was the secondary back that eventually gave tufted carpeting its status as a quality product, and eliminated forever the "bedspread" connotation.

The United States embargo of mainland China in the early 1950s cut off a major source of carpet wool, but synthetic fibers quickly took wool's place. Although there is a whole range of synthetic fibers and yarns, nylon is the most notable because of its strength, durability,

83. Tufting machinery. (Courtesy of West Point Pepperell, Carpet and Rug Division of Cabin Crafts, Inc., Dalton, Georgia.)

and — perhaps most important — its ability to take color. Nylon carpets can be tufted and then dyed, whereas most other synthetics must be dyed before being tufted. Today, some two-thirds of all carpeting in this country is tufted of nylon yarns.

In addition to plain and multicolored cut and looped pile fabrics, embossed designs with areas of high and low pile can be produced by adding several types of pattern mechanisms (figure 84). Tufted carpets may also be silk-screened (figure 85). Many firms have maintained contact with the past by handmaking special-order carpeting with a single-needle handgun (figures 86 and 87).

Wiltons and Axminsters continue to be woven commercially on a small scale (figure 88). Meanwhile, there is a new development: machine-knitting carpets. This process began about 1940 and attained commercial success about 1950. Since then there have been many rapid technologic advances, but knitted carpets account for only a small proportion of the total carpet production. They are made of a warp-knitted fabric composed of warp chains, wefting, and pile warps. The knitting is done in a single operation by a machine known as a double-needle bar knitter (figure 89).

Other experimental types of carpetmaking that have been attempted, most without

84. A modern hand-tufted
wool carpet. "Marco Polo" designed by Stanislav V'soske.
(Courtesy of V'soske, New
York, New York.)

85. A modern screen-printed
tufted carpet. (Courtesy of
Wellco Carpets, Calhoun,
Georgia.)

86. Custom rug being made with a hand-tufting gun. (Courtesy of West Point Pepperell, Carpet and Rug Division of Cabin Crafts, Inc., Dalton, Georgia.)

87. A modern 1-ply hand-tufted carpet designed by Charles Counts and manufactured by Ronald Everett of Rising Fawn, Georgia. (Photograph by Edward DuPuy.)

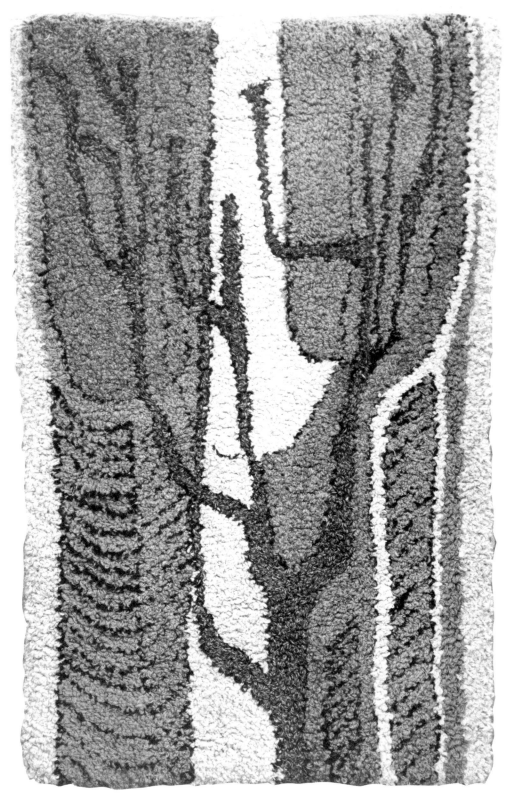

88. A modern Axminster carpet, "The American Legend Wall Rug" by Alexander Smith Carpets, Mohasco Corporation, Amsterdam, New York. A bicentennial patriotic design of eagle, liberty bell, and flag in 24 colors.

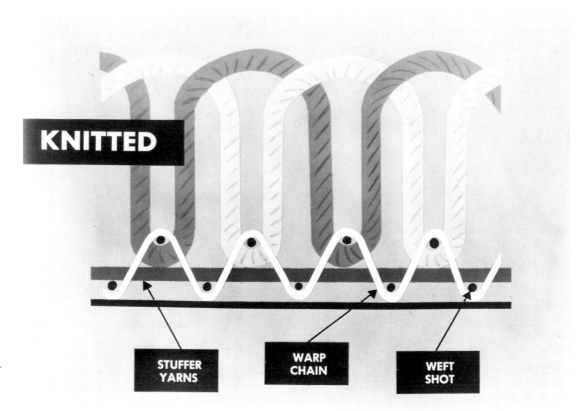

KNITTED

STUFFER YARNS **WARP CHAIN** **WEFT SHOT**

89. Diagram of a modern knitted carpet construction. (Courtesy of the Carpet and Rug Institute, Dalton, Georgia.)

commercial success, include imbedding, flocking, or otherwise attaching or impregnating fibers to a base material. Meanwhile, carpet printing gained great impetus after 1960 with the development of silk-screen machinery in Austria and West Germany. These machines can print permanent colors on all types of fibers and weaves. By 1975, approximately 20 percent of the American carpets were printed as more and more colors and textured effects became possible.

As the modern American carpet industry has grown, there has also been a revival of handcrafts—including rugs. Individual weaver-artists are creating both traditional and experimental rugs. Such groups as the Navahos have revived a traditional craft. Handcrafts have also had their effect on the industry. In the 1930s and 1940s weaver Anni Albers, wife of the late artist Joseph Albers, influenced many budding fabric designers at Black Mountain College in North Carolina. She made a major contribution toward bringing design and industry into harmony. In the 1940s and 1950s such designers as Dorothy Liebes of San Francisco and New York opened the door to bright colors and simple textural effects being used in mass production. Today, such artists as weaver-designer Glen Kaufman of the University of Georgia continue that tradition, making both fine-art pieces and designing for industry (figure 91). In addition, highly experimental work such as the "environmental" rugs of Urban Jupena of the University of Michigan is undertaken (figure 92). The future of the art of rugmaking, both industrial and handcrafted, may be as bright and intriguing as has been its past.

90. Detail of a contemporary reproduction of a nineteenth-century ingrain carpet from the Metropolitan Museum of Art collection by Scalamandré of New York. Colors are orange, beige, green, and red. See Technical Analysis section. (Courtesy of Scalamandré.)

91. Modern handmade rug by Glen Kaufman, University of Georgia, who says of his work: "The rug has no specific design origin although landscapes, lunarscapes, comets, and a host of other unidentifiable influences come into play. I strive for richness in color and texture by selecting yarns varying in size, construction, type of wool and color characteristics. I have employed slit tapestry and eccentric weft techniques to achieve a shape that breaks away from the traditional rectilinear carpet."

OPPOSITE:

92. "Crevice," a modern handwoven "environmental" sculptured rug by Urban Jupena, Detroit, Michigan. Jupena's work is highly experimental; he says of it: "To me a rug is a mirror of the earth's surface, done in soft man-made fiber, rather than hard stone . . . The inspiration for this rug was found in the weather-beaten craggy rocks along the coast of Maine which have been carved by the elements of wind and water. A rug of this nature creates a natural environment for a person to live in, without the dampness and discomfort of real rock." See Technical Analysis section. (Photograph by Bob Vigility.)

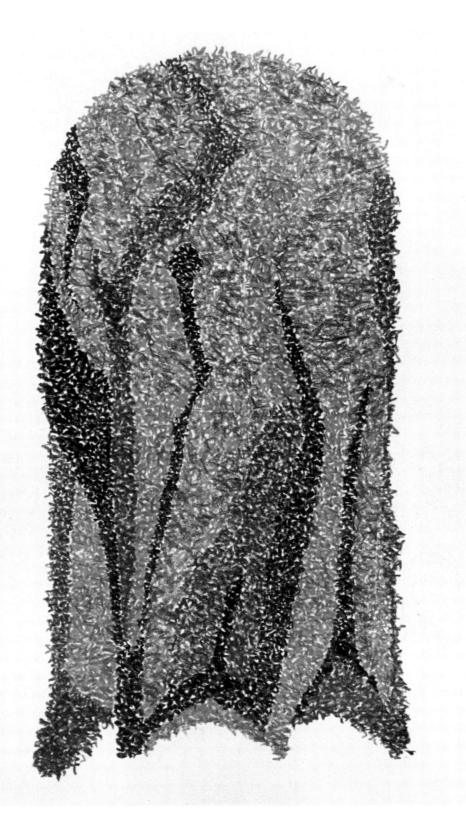

Notes

For complete source, see Bibliography

1. Cole-Williamson, p. 4.
2. As quoted in Roth, p. 48.
3. As reported in Little, p. 4.
4. Cole-Williamson, p. 4.
5. Roth, p. 26.
6. Ibid., pp. 26-27.
7. Ibid., p. 28.
8. Ibid., pp. 27-28.
9. Ibid., p. 28.
10. As quoted in Roth, p. 29.
11. Roth, p. 27.
12. Little, p. 28.
13. Ibid., pp. 24-25.
14. Comstock, p. 48.
15. Little, pp. 17-19.
16. As quoted in Roth, pp. 12-13.
17. Little, p. 24.
18. As quoted in Roth, p. 12, and Little, p. 19.
19. Roth, p. 10.
20. Ibid., pp. 22-23.
21. Ibid., p. 23.
22. As quoted in Little, p. 24.
23. Roth, p. 24.
24. Ibid., p. 26.
25. Little, p. 22.
26. Roth, p. 18.
27. Little, p. 21.
28. Little, p. 62, figure 24.
29. As quoted in Roth, p. 17.
30. Ibid., p. 14.
31. Little, pp. 22-24.
32. As reported in Little, p. 23.
33. Roth, p. 12.
34. Ibid., p. 12.
35. Ibid., p. 22.
36. Little, pp. 22-23.
37. Ibid., p. 17.
38. Lanier, p. 40.
39. McMullan, p. 221.

40. Tattersall-Reed, p. 24.
41. Landreau, in press, 1976.
42. Cole-Williamson, p. 4.
43. McMullan, p. 221.
44. Roth, p. 4.
45. Ibid., p. 7.
46. Ibid., p. 7.
47. Ibid., p. 9-10.
48. McMullan, p. 221.
49. Tattersall-Reed, p. 28.
50. McMullan, p. 221.
51. Ibid., p. 221.
52. Lanier, pp. 96-102.
53. Dimand-Mailey, pp. 192-194.
54. Landreau, in press, 1976.
55. Kenyon, figure 1.
56. Landreau-Pickering, pp. 12-15; Emery, pp. 221-228.
57. Kühnel-Bellinger, pp. 53-58.
58. Erdmann (1970), pp. 205-208.
59. Tattersall-Reed, p. 28.
60. Ibid., p. 27.
61. Ibid., pp. 27-28.
62. McMullan, p. 221; Tattersall-Reed, p. 29.
63. Cole-Williamson, p. 33.
64. Roth, p. 44.
65. Little, p. 32.
66. Roth, p. 45 and figure 21.
67. Landreau-Pickering, p. 16.
68. Ibid., p. 8.
69. Mera, p. 82.
70. Lanier, pp. 34-35.
71. Little, pp. 27-28.
72. Lanier, pp. 34-35.
73. Roth, p. 47.
74. Cole-Williamson, p. 31.
75. Ibid., p. 31.
76. Little, p. 32.
77. Ibid., p. 33.

78. Ibid., p. 33.
79. Ibid. pp. 34-35.
80. Ibid., p. 36.
81. Ibid., p. 36.
82. Little, p. 79.
83. Cole-Williamson, pp. 36-40.
84. Page 28.
85. Lanier, p. 31.
86. Roth, p. 33, figure 15.
87. Ibid., pp. 29-35.
88. Cole-Williamson, p. 11.
89. Bigelow-Hartford, pp. 46-52
90. Cole-Williamson, p. 257.
91. As quoted in Cole-Williamson, p. 21.
92. Cole-Williamson, p. 32.
93. Roth, pp. 35-37.
94. Cole-Williamson, p. 12.
95. Roth, p. 37.
96. As quoted in Roth, p. 40.
97. Cole-Williamson, pp. 63-65.
98. Emery, pp. 78-79.
99. Cole-Williamson, p. 68.
100. Ibid., chapter 4.
101. Ibid., p. 103.
102. *Carpets and Rugs* (Hoover Company) figure 3.
103. Ibid., p. 25.

Technical Analysis For
Floor Coverings in the Exhibition

S and Z indicate direction of spin, see Emery, pages 9-12. Author's structural terminology in general follows Emery.

Figures 6 and 8.   Floorcloth reproduction from Floorcloths, Inc., Annapolis, Maryland.   5′ x 7′.   Heavy cotton canvas, about No. 9, weight 2/2 balanced twill.   Warp: 5 yarns Z-spun, plied S.   Weft: 4 Z-spun yarns plied S.   Yarn count: Approximately 19 warps and 16 wefts per 2.5 cm (1 inch).

Figure 23.   "Transylvanian" rug, Textile Museum (cat. no. R34.21.3).   Wool.   1.72 m high x 1.28 m wide.   Turkish knot, 2 rows of ground weft between rows of knots.   Warp: 2 Z-spun, plied S.   Weft: Z-spun.   Knot count: 7 horizontal x 8 vertical/2.5 cm; 56 knots to square 2.5 cm (1 inch).   No selvedge.   End finish: warp ends cut.   Analysis from Ann Hedlund, Textile Museum.

Figure 24.   Bergama district rug, Textile Museum (cat. no. R34.2.4).   Wool.   1.56 m high x 1.675 m wide.   Turkish knot, 2 and 4 rows of ground weft between rows of knots.   Warp: 2 Z spun, plied S.   Weft: Z-spun.   Pile weft: 2 Z-spun, unplied.   Knot count: 6.5 horizontal x 11 vertical per 2.5 cm; 71-72 knots to square 2.5 cm (1 inch).   End finish: warp ends cut, fringe 3 cm.   Analysis from Ann Hedlund, Textile Museum.

Figure 34.   Turkey work, Colonial Williamsburg (no. 1954.375).   Technical analysis of this rug published in Lanier, p. 6.

Figure 39.   Needlework rug, Colonial Williamsburg (no. 1956.45).   Technical analysis of this rug published in Lanier, p. 22.

Figure 40.   Tapestry floorcloth, Colonial Williamsburg (no. 1956.537).   Technical analysis of this rug published in Lanier, p. 42.

Figure 41.   Navaho rug, twentieth century, Carnegie Institute, Museum of Natural History.   Wool.   6′11″ high x 3′9½″ wide.   Dovetailed tapestry, braided on all four sides.

Figure 45.   Kentucky rag rug, by Sylvia Spradlin.   4′9″ high x 3′ wide.   Plain weave.   Warp: cotton, commercial, plied S.   Weft: woolen cloth scraps and thick yarn.   Plain weave ends, hemmed, coarse weave.

Figure 46.   Venetian carpeting fragment, Smithsonian Institution (cat. no. T.4908).   Wool.   15 cm high x 102 cm wide.   Plain weave, warp-faced.   Warp: 2 Z-spun, plied S.   Weft: 2 Z-spun, plied S.   Yarn count: 23 warps and 10-11 wefts per 2.5 cm (1 inch).   No selvedges or ends.   Yellows, reds, browns, 2 greens.

Figure 65.   Ingrain carpeting, Smithsonian Institution (cat. no. T.7429). 31 cm high x 55 cm wide.   Handwoven ingrain, double-cloth (2-ply) Jacquard pattern.   Warp: 2 Z-spun, plied S in brown, tan, and white cotton.   Weft: Z-spun dark brown wool; 2 Z-spun unplied wool in light red, tan, yellow; at top, 4 rows of 2 Z-spun plied S in tan cotton.   Yarn count: 10 wefts (1 set of 2) and 12 warps (1 set of 2) per 2.5 cm (1 inch).   One complete selvedge.

Figure 66.   Wool carpeting, Smithsonian Institution (cat. no. T.16934).   66 cm high x 91-92 cm wide. Double-cloth, 2-ply.   Warp: 2 Z-spun, plied S (2 sets in 4 sections; brown-white, green-red, brown-white, green red).   Weft: 2 S-spun in black, dark brown, red-brown, tan, red-tan, red, light red, dark red, white, olive green, blue-green, dark green, green. Yarn count: 13 wefts (1 set of 2) and 14 warps (1 set of 2) per 2.5 cm (1 inch). Plain selvedge, hemmed at both ends.

Figure 67. Ingrain carpeting, Smithsonian Institution (cat. no. T.7419). Wool. 196 cm high x 91 cm wide. Double-cloth, 2-ply. Yarn count: 15 wefts (1 set of 2) and 16 warps (1 set of 2) per 2.5 cm (1 inch). Plain selvedge.

Figure 68. Wool carpeting, Smithsonian Institution (cat. no. T.11395, Patent 104,232). 82 cm high x 91 cm wide. 2-ply ingrain, double-weave, of a type sometimes called damask carpeting. Warp: 2 Z-spun. Weft: 2 Z-spun, plied S. Yarn count: 16 warps (1 set of 2) and 13 wefts (1 set of 2) per 2.5 cm (1 inch). Plain selvedge, cut warp ends.

Figure 69. Wool carpeting, Smithsonian Institution (cat. no. T.11395, Patent 142,681). 25-29 cm high x 55-56 cm wide. Double-cloth (2-ply) with "damask" (compound warp float weave) border. Warp: 2 Z-spun, plied S. Weft: 2 Z-spun, plied S. Yarn count: 16 warps (1 set of 2) and 15 wefts (1 set of 2) per 2.5 cm (1 inch). Plain selvedge, cut ends. Center colors: red and grey. Border colors: white, brown, green, yellow, red, and orange.

Figure 70. Carpeting, Smithsonian Institution (cat. no. T.11395, Patent 574,023). 120 cm high x 91 cm wide. Compound-weave (2-ply), ingrain woven in a design imitating Brussels carpeting. Warp: 2 Z-spun, plied S in brown wool. Weft: Z-spun, alternating single- and paired-wool; at ends 2 Z-spun, plied S in cotton. Yarn count: 14 wefts (1 set of 2) per 2.5 cm (1 inch). Colors: Green and brown, white, light blue and gold.

Figure 71. Wool carpeting, Smithsonian Institution (cat. no. T.7415). 191 cm. high x 89 cm wide. Triple-cloth (3-ply) ingrain, Jacquard woven. Warp: 2 Z-spun, plied S. Weft: 2 Z-spun, plied S. Yarn count: 50 warps (total) and 12-13 wefts (1 set of 3) per 2.5 cm (1 inch). Colors: red, brown, white, green.

Figure 72. Wool carpeting, Smithsonian Institution (cat. no. T.11448). 132 cm high x 2 widths sewn together, 60 cm each. Triple-cloth (3-ply) ingrain, Jacquard woven. Warp: 2

Z-spun, plied S. Weft: 2 S and S-spun (ocher). Yarn count: 12 warps (1 set of 3) and 13 wefts (1 set of 3) per 2.5 cm (1 inch). Hemmed.

Figure 76. Wilton sampler, Merrimack Valley Textile Museum (cat. no. 64.46). Analysis courtesy of Katherine R. Koob, Merrimack Valley Textile Museum: "... specifications are 220 per inch in the warp (180 colored [6 colors of 30 each] worsted 2 ply S twist; 20 cotton 4 ply blue grey S twist; 20 cotton 3 ply grey S twist) and 1 cotton 5 ply Z twist serving as end thread in both selvedges. 39 weft per inch, cotton 3 ply grey S twist. 3 colored threads per tuft—10 tufts per inch in the warp, 13 tufts per inch in the weft=130 tufts per inch. An extra warp of 7 cotton 3 ply threads is used to weave Whittall Anglo Persian on the back. Pile is ¼ inch deep and cut." See write-up on the 3-shot weave in the legend of figure 76. Five rods are used to hold looped pile until cut. Warp ends at bottom are tied in the sampler. Overall dimensions: 27¼" wide x 18¼" high (cloth) plus 9" (unwoven warp) and 7" (sampler board at top)—total 34½" high.

Figure 78. Brussels carpet, Smithsonian (cat. no. T.7399). 93-94 cm high x 70 cm wide. Warp loop pile (Brussels), Jacquard woven. Ground warp: blue-grey 2 Z-spun, plied S. Pattern warp (5 sets): 2 Z-spun, plied S in wool. Weft: Z-spun in pinkish linen (?). Yarn count 18-20 ground warps 2.5 cm (1 inch). Pile colors: red (background), black (outlines), yellow, green, blue, pale yellow and dark red together. Plain selvedge, cut ends.

Figure 90. Wool reproduction by Scalamandré. Design no. 97358. 3'3" x 3'. 2/26 warp, 2/20 weft, 4-ply. 36 warps x 26 wefts per inch. 36" wide fabric, 40" repeat. Shuttles are changed by hand due to large variety of weft colors.

Figure 91. Rug by Glen Kaufman. Turkish (Gordes) knot pile. 44" x 84". Warp, plied S linen. Weft, plied S wool. Pile weft plied S wools (about 30 different yarns). Colors: browns, tans, purples, violets, and greys. Information supplied by the artist.

Figure 92. Modern handmade rug by Urban Jupena. Turkish knots, Z-spun rug-weaving wool. Used over foam pillows and forms.

Bibliography

Bigelow-Hartford Carpet Company. *A Century of Carpet and Rug Making in America, 1825-1925.* New York, 1925. Written by and for the Bigelow-Hartford Carpet Company. Not well documented.

Bode, Wilhelm von, and Ernst Kühnel. *Antique Rugs from the Near East.* English translation by Charles Grant Ellis. Berlin, 1958. There is also a 1970 English edition published by Klinkhardt and Biermann, Berlin. One of the most important texts on the early history of Oriental carpets.

Carpets and Rugs. North Canton, Ohio: The Hoover Company, 1966. A commercial effort, but it has some useful statistics.

Christensen, Erwin O. *The Index of American Design.* Washington, D.C.: The Smithsonian Institution, 1950. Useful for illustrations of paintings with rugs in them.

Cole, Arthur, and Harold Williamson. *The American Carpet Manufacture: A History and an Analysis.* Cambridge: Harvard University Press, 1941. The best history of the nineteenth-century American carpet industry.

Comstock, Helen. "Eighteenth-Century Floor Cloths." Antiques, vol. 67, no. 1 (January 1955). Short text on painted and stenciled cloths. Augments the Roth text.

Dimand, M. S., and Jean Mailey. *Oriental Rugs in the Metropolitan Museum of Art.* New York: New York Graphics Society, 1973. Catalog of the Metropolitan's collection. There are illustrations of types of Oriental rugs found in early America.

Emery, Irene. *The Primary Structures of Fabrics.* Washington, D.C.: The Textile Museum, 1966. The basic text on textile structures of all kinds, including rugs. My technology is based on Emery.

Erdmann, Kurt. *Oriental Carpets: An Essay on their History.* English translation by Charles Grant Ellis, London: A. Zwemmer, Ltd., 1960. Along with Bode-Kühnel, the Erdmann translations are the most important works on early Oriental rug history.

———. *Seven Hundred Years of Oriental Carpets.* English translation by M. H. Beattie and H. Herzog; Hanna Erdmann, ed. Berkeley and Los Angeles: University of California Press, 1970. This is perhaps the most readable of the good texts on early oriental rugs and is still available.

Ewing, John S., and Nancy P. Norton. *Broadlooms and Businessmen: A History of the Bigelow-Sanford Carpet Company.* New York, 1955. A company produced effort. Updates the Bigelow-Hartford book, of 1925, but is not well documented.

Irene Emery Roundtable on Museum Textiles, 1975 Proceedings. Patricia L. Fiske, ed. In press, 1976, by The Textile Museum, Washington, D.C. Roundtable for 1975 had discussions by several authorities — Lanier, Patridge, Hummel — on American floor coverings.

Kenyon, Otis Allen. *Carpets and Rugs.* North Canton, Ohio: The Hoover Company, 1923. Early history of the American industry, but not as thorough as Cole.

Kühnel, Ernest, and Louise Bellinger. *Catalogue of Spanish Rugs.* Washington, D.C.: The Textile Museum, 1953. The basic book on Spanish rugs.

Landreau, Anthony, and W. R. Pickering. *From the Bosporus to Samarkand: Flat-Woven Rugs,* Washington, D.C.: The Textile Museum, 1969. First text on flat-woven rugs from the Middle East.

Landreau, Anthony, and Wendy Hefford. *Rugs Around the World*. In press, 1976, by Helvetica Press, New York. Summation of rug studies and history.

Lanier, Mildred B. *English and Oriental Carpets at Williamsburg*. Williamsburg, Virginia: Colonial Williamsburg, 1975. Excellent, well-documented catalogue raisonné of the Williamsburg carpet collection. A basic text on American floor coverings.

Lipman, Jean, and Alice Winchester. *The Flowering of American Folk Art, 1776-1876*. New York: Viking Press, 1974. Useful for some illustrations of carpets and carpets in paintings.

Little, Nina Fletcher. *Floor Coverings in New England Before 1850*. Old Sturbridge Village, Massachusetts, 1967. Along with Roth and Lanier, this is one of the most important texts on American floor coverings. Well documented and illustrated.

Martin, Fredrik R. *A History of Oriental Carpets before 1800*. Vienna, 1908. One of the earliest rug books. Pioneered in the historic approach to rug studies.

McMullan, Joseph V. "The Turkey Carpet in Early America." *Antiques*, vol. 65, no. 3 (March 1954), p. 220. First article written about Oriental rugs in America.

————. *Islamic Carpets*. New York: Near East Research Center, 1965. Several carpets similar to those found in America are illustrated. See references in my text.

Mera, H. P. *Navajo Textile Arts*. With additions by Roger and Jean Moss. Santa Barbara and Salt Lake City: Peregrine Smith, Inc., 1975.

Robinson, George. *Carpets*. 2d rev. ed. Worcester and London: Trinity Press, 1972. Industrial carpet book; useful for technological descriptions.

Roth, Rodris. "Floor Coverings in 18th-Century America." Paper 59 in *Contributions from the Museum of History and Technology (United States National Museum Bulletin*, 250) by various authors. Washington, D.C.: Smithsonian Institution, 1967. The basic text on American floor coverings — early history — thoroughly researched and documented. My text merely updates it.

Tattersall, C.E.C. *A History of British Carpets*. Revised by S. Reed. Leigh-on-Sea, England: F. Lewis, 1966. A basic text. Outlines the early Axminster history.